OFF-BEAT

What's it like to sleep in Grand Central Station for ten years? . . . Practice golf shots on Eleventh Avenue at two in the morning? . . . Save bums from jail by stealing them from the police? . . . Stay in a hotel without money? . . . Flourish in New York City without a job, without a home, without friends?

Here are the amazing, bizarre, incredible, hilarious, true stories of people who live without money and like it. A strange breed of off-beat characters, they inhabit a city New Yorkers seldom see.

"Fascinating."　—*New York Herald Tribune*

"A charming, diverting, and warm book."
　　　　　　—*Chicago Sunday Tribune*

"Not a line but pulls you forward, deeper into the twilight where Mr. Love's people live. You find yourself, even in your own snug apartment, suddenly among incredible folk . . . real people."　　　　—*New York Times*

THIS IS A REPRINT OF THE HARDCOVER EDITION ORIGINALLY PUBLISHED BY HARCOURT, BRACE & COMPANY

SUBWAYS ARE FOR
SLEEPING

Edmund G. Love

A SIGNET BOOK

Published by The New American Library

To Anne

Published as a SIGNET BOOK
by arrangement with Harcourt, Brace & World, Inc.,
who have authorized this softcover edition.
A hardcover edition is available from
Harcourt, Brace & World, Inc.

FIRST PRINTING, NOVEMBER, 1958
SIXTH PRINTING, DECEMBER, 1962

Subways Are for Sleeping is published in England by
Victor Gollancz, Ltd.

The names of all persons and hotels have been
changed. In some instances, to protect an
individual or his family or his friends, the
exact locale of an incident has been disguised.

SIGNET BOOKS are published by
The New American Library of World Literature, Inc.
501 Madison Avenue, New York 22, New York

PRINTED IN THE UNITED STATES OF AMERICA

Contents

Introduction

Not long ago, New York papers reported that seven old ladies had been found who lived in the rest rooms at Pennsylvania Station. They had lived there for three months. The judge who heard their case and the reporters who wrote about it seemed surprised that such a thing was possible. It is not only possible, but the accepted way of life in certain social circles. I know of two men who have been living in Grand Central station for almost ten years. They have learned to vary their routine enough to maintain the anonymity necessary for such a project. Unlike the seven old ladies, they have not been found.

When the fine documentary movie *On the Bowery* opened, a great many people said it was exaggerated, that people simply could not live as these men lived.

In writing this book, I came to realize a long time ago that some persons may not believe that my people exist either. Often successful people are intolerant of less fortunate individuals. In an age protected by Social Security and unemployment insurance, by prosperity, and organizations like Alcoholics Anonymous, it seems inconceivable that a person can still be lost.

A few years ago I was caught up in a whirlwind of my own. When it all ended, I found myself walking the streets. I needed more than just a job. I needed to reassess life. Something, somewhere, had gone wrong. I may have listened wrong. I may have thought wrong. Or, I could have been right and the world wrong. It seemed to me, at the time, that the reassessment was more important than the material side of things. I had to think. I had to have time to think. So I drifted. I remember a long series of days and weeks during which I slept on the sofas in the apartments of friends. I recall that during one whole winter month I went down to the Hospital for Special Surgery every afternoon at two o'clock to call on a girl who was confined there. I hardly knew her, but the hospital was warm and I was cold. This may sound hard-boiled, but by that time I'd found out that necessity takes precedence over nicety. I bought a tablet and a pencil and sat on a bench in Grand Central, trying to write and think there.

I say all this because I want it understood that I did not drop into this world of which I write simply to study it. I was there because I couldn't seem to escape it. My rehabilitation, if it can be called that, was a long drawn-out process because it involved a complete change in my thinking as well as a simple economic readjustment. In some ways, it is still going forward. I worked intermittently at a wide variety of jobs. I did not stay in New York, but I did return to the city two or three times. I met a lot of people and I learned a lot of things. More than once I had a stranger suggest to me a place to eat, or a place to sleep, or a place to keep warm. I learned a hundred ways to pick up a dollar or two. I consider this knowledge important, but I learned something even more valuable. I learned a lot about human beings.

A few years ago, in writing about a group of people who spent virtually all their time in restaurants, Cholly Knickerbocker coined the term Café Society. In my wanderings I became conscious of an entirely different kind of society— a group of people who live, by and large, by their wits. They are people of ingenuity who do not conform to the patterns of life which "sound" people prescribe. Most of them have no regular job; only a few of them have a normal home. They live on the fringes of our cities. Many people are not conscious of their existence at all, yet, once I had been thrust into their midst, I had no trouble recognizing them at once. Fifty-five years ago, O. Henry used to wander the streets of New York, searching them out. He loved them and he appreciated their absurdities. Damon Runyon wrote most of his short stories about them. I have found them in cities other than New York, but in no other city except New York have I found the same ingenuity. New York attracts the most talented people in the world in the arts and professions. It also attracts them in other fields. Even the bums are talented.

But these people I write about are not really bums. The big difference between them and the real, down-and-out bum could be called a matter of hope. I recognize in them something of what I felt myself. Most of them are in a state of reassessment. They have come up against something which they cannot understand, and which they want to think about. The thinking is important to them. My people still believe in miracles. Your average bum does not. He has given up hope. Most of my people are living stop-gap lives. They are waiting for the big break. That break may be a call from the producer of a Broadway show. It may be a horse that gallops home at 40-1. It may be just a bright and shining light that suddenly comes to show them the way out of the jungle. Some aren't sure what kind of a break they are waiting for, but they have assured me that they will recognize it when it comes. In the meantime, they wait and try to keep going through today, for tomorrow may bring the miracle. Tomorrow is always the big day.

This is not a sociological or psychiatric study. These are stories about people that I have come to know. One of them has been a friend of mine for twelve years, another for less than a year. Most of them I have known for four or five years. I know all their stories from beginning to end, but I do not think it is necessary to dwell on the circumstances, real or imagined, that brought them where they are. One thing is important to know—they can be trusted and believed. Sometimes they are thoroughly exasperating. Sometimes they are funny without meaning to be. Sometimes they exhibit a sense of humor or an understanding of life that is amazing. They accept other people on the terms the others lay down, never on their own. If someone is contemptuous of them, they are contemptuous in return. If someone is indifferent, they ignore him. If someone is friendly, he may get the shirt off a back that really needs it. These people can be selfish, grasping, crooked, and hard-boiled at one moment, and completely unselfish the next. It is response for response.

They are the most observant people I have ever known. They spot little things and learn to use them, whether it be the foibles of human nature or the contents of a trash can. They exploit their environment as craftily and as thoroughly as Robinson Crusoe ever did. They are masters of ingenuity. Most people would find it impossible to get along in a big city, day after day, with little or no money, yet most of these do it constantly. They can be good managers, they can be persistent, and they can be as patient as the situation demands. The most certainly are not lazy. All of them work hard. Some live in such a frenzy of activity that one wonders how long they can keep going. While they are eminently unsuccessful in conventional terms, they are successful in their own. Are they wrong or is society wrong in measuring and judging these people? There are ministers who think that the efforts of saloon keepers are misdirected, and, I might add, vice versa.

These people are like the man who takes a short cut, gets lost, and then explores the countryside, forgetting completely why he took the short cut in the first place. All of them have built their improbable lives to furnish temporary security until they can achieve their goals. As time has passed, they have become attached to their way of life. It gives them real security. They become afraid to leave something they are sure of. To them there is more security in a home on a fire escape or in a job washing windows than there is in a furnished apartment or a regular job. An apartment might burn down. A man with a regular job might get laid off.

I have been asked if it is possible to reform these people. I couldn't change them. I doubt if anyone could. If there is any change at all it must come from within themselves. All of them are wrestling, consciously or unconsciously, with problems. Until the solutions are apparent, they want to be allowed to solve them in their own way. They think that criticism from others is unjustified and an unwarranted invasion of their privacy. While they may recognize that their way of life is not entirely conventional, they have long ago excused it to themselves. Therefore it is not wrong to them. They withdraw from criticism, shunning the people who offer it. They appear to be anti-social, when they are not at all. If a person can give them warmth and understanding rather than disapproval, they accept gladly. They recognize friendship as the only true charity. A person who gives them a dime, and tells them how to use it is not giving anything at all. He is buying something. No one wants to be bought.

I think the best indication of the true nature of my friends is the fact that they have not turned to vicious crime to solve their problems. They have regard for others. They seem to accept their lot with cheerfulness and a determination to get along, somehow, until things get better. They have no self-pity, a rather common trait among true bums. Indeed, I think my people have a simpler and more profound faith than society as a whole. I have never met one who did not believe that some outside force controls and guides his life. He may call it Fate, he may call it Luck, or he may call it God, but he believes in it, and he believes in it so implicitly that it governs his life. He believes in its basic goodness. The material results may be continually disappointing, but everything will come out all right in the end. This is a lesson that I learned. It is a lesson that all of these, my friends, have learned. I am sure they would join with me in hoping that others learn it too. Their philosophy does not depend upon material things, or upon a well-ordered universe. They accept the bad with the good, the improbable with the probable. They have accepted themselves.

These are my friends. I would like you to know them.

Subways Are for Sleeping

On March 4, 1953, at approximately 11:30 P.M., Henry Shelby walked into the New York City hotel where he had maintained an apartment for five months. Upon asking for his key at the desk, he was informed by the clerk that he had been locked out until such time as his bill was settled. The bill amounted to about $113. At the moment, Shelby had about $14, no job, and no friends upon whom he felt free to call for help. Without any argument, he turned and walked back out the door.

In the time that has passed since that night, he has returned to the hotel only once, and then merely to see if he had any mail. He has not attempted to retrieve any of his belongings held by the management. With the exception of approximately three and one-half months, in the summer of 1953, he has been one of the thousands of men in various stages of vagrancy who wander the streets of New York City at all hours of the day and night.

I met Henry Shelby in Greenwich Village three years ago. Since that time I have spent many evenings with him over a drink talking about philosophy, about world problems—and our own. Henry Shelby, today, is forty-one years old, but looks at least five years younger. He is five feet, eleven and one-half inches tall, weighs 162 pounds. His hair is black but thinning, and his eyes are a deep blue. He has no disfigurements, and his bearing is good. The key to his personality lies in his eyes, which express the depth of his feeling or a quiet humor, depending upon his mood. When he is deep in thought or troubled, he is apt to trace patterns on the floor or in the dirt with the toe of his shoe. At other times he moves briskly and with some of the grace and sureness of an athlete.

He is a graduate of the University of Michigan with a master's degree in economics. He also holds a life teacher's certificate in the state of Michigan and was, at one time, a teacher in the public schools of Lansing. His master's degree studies were concentrated in the field of accounting procedure, and for four years after World II, he was an accountant with the Post Office Department in Washington. His associates there consider him an excellent man in his field, and at least two of them say that he could probably qualify as a certified public accountant. In addition to these qualifications, he is experienced and capable in the field of public relations, where his approach has been described as "fresh" and "honest."

The city of New York has long been noted for the number and variety of its vagrants. Estimates as to the number of homeless and penniless men and women run from a conservative 10,000 to somewhere around half a million. Vagrants in other parts of the United States are a migratory lot, usually moving with the weather, but the New York variety stays put, occupying park benches, flophouses, gutters, and doorways in all seasons. There are many who possess qualifications as rich as Henry Shelby's. There are many who are literally human derelicts living out their days in a drunken stupor, waiting for an obscure death in the river or a ward at Bellevue. In between, there are as many gradations as there are strata in normal society. Almost the only things all vagrants have in common are a hard-luck story and an air of bewilderment. Not all of them have lost hope.

Henry Shelby is not a hopeless man, but he is certainly bewildered. He himself describes his present life as treading water, waiting to see how things come out. "In the meantime," he told me, "I'm getting along all right. I'm perfectly happy."

In his months as a vagrant he has become an expert at management and has learned to put first things first. In his case this means food, cleanliness, and shelter, in that order. He prides himself on the fact that he has never panhandled, never visited a soup kitchen or taken a night's lodging in one of the various hostels maintained by charitable agencies in the city. He has accepted handouts, but he can recall only one instance where anyone ever stepped up to him and gave him money: One night in the middle of winter he noticed advertisements for the *première* of a motion picture at a Broadway theater. He arrived early and took up a prominent position against the ropes under the marquee. As he stood there, watching the celebrities arrive in their limousines, a man came over to him and placed an unfolded ten-dollar- bill in his hand.

Shelby has never been completely penniless except for one very brief period when he left New York. He has set fifteen cents, which represents subway fare, as the absolute minimum below which he will not allow his finances to sink. He has no maximum, but rarely possesses more than thirty dollars, which represents about one week's salary at present minimum levels. He acquires his money in a variety of ways. He is able to pick up a day's work here and there, carrying sandwich boards, working as a roustabout on the waterfront, washing dishes in cheap restaurants, or shoveling snow for the city.

When he gets money, he nurses it carefully. He can tell, one minute after he gets it, exactly how long it will last, because he knows what he's going to eat, how many cigarettes he is going to smoke, and the amount it will cost him for lodging and incidentals. There are no extras in his life.

Virtually all of Shelby's cash goes for food and cigarettes. His breakfasts, invariably, consist of a glass of fruit or vegetable juice; his lunches, of a sandwich, usually a frank-furter, and a glass of milk. His one substantial meal is supper, and into it he piles all the dietary necessities he has missed since he last ate such a meal. His plate is apt to be loaded with green vegetables, cooked vegetables, and meat. He will haggle back and forth with the counterman in order to get these items, usually trading off potatoes and dessert for them. He never looks at the contents of a meal until he looks at the prices and he always chooses the cheapest meal on the menu, unless it contains sea food, which he detests. He knows where all the best food bargains in town are to be found. A bargain means quantity, but once or twice a week he will seek out a place that serves something of which he is especially fond.

Between meals he drinks coffee, usually two cups during the morning and three cups during the afternoon and evening. When he is especially broke he cuts out regular meals and subsists entirely on coffee, loading all the sugar and cream he can into his cup. He explains that these are free calories, and that calories, no matter what form they take, will keep him going until he is able to eat regularly again.

Shelby says that the truest statement he has ever heard is that no one will ever starve to death in the United States, and his technique for getting food when he is low on money is a simple one. He walks the streets until he finds a restaurant with a sign in the window that reads "dish-washer wanted," or "counterman wanted." He goes in and works long enough to pay for a meal and earn a little extra money. Usually he completes whatever constitutes a full day's work, but if the restaurant is a pleasant place, if he is treated well and the food is good, he may stay a week, or even longer. He is a good worker and is well liked by his bosses and fellow employees. Many of the latter are men like himself.

He has learned a lot of odd jobs around kitchens and has filled in as a chef at two cafeterias, and as a short-order cook at a counter restaurant. At one place where he worked for five weeks, the manager recommended him for the managership of another unit in the chain which had fallen vacant. In this particular restaurant Shelby can always be sure of a job of some kind when he is broke; the manager will put him to work washing windows if there is nothing else available. The same condition holds true at five or six other places in town, but Shelby never uses them unless he is really desperate. He refers to them humorously as his social security.

Shelby usually allots no more than fifteen cents a day for shelter. Occasionally he pays more than this, but only when he has gotten by for two or three days without spending anything extra. Shelter means a place to sleep to Shelby, nothing else. His great preference, month in and month out, is for the Sixth and Eighth Avenue subways. He very rarely sleeps on the IRT or BMT. The IRT, with its ramshackle, noisy cars, is uncomfortable. The BMT has suitable accommodations, but, as Shelby describes it, "an undesirable clientele."

Shelby usually boards the Eighth Avenue subway at Pennsylvania Station between midnight and one in the morning and takes the first express that comes along. At that hour there is usually a seat, especially in the front car, and he immediately settles down and drops off to sleep.

He has developed the happy faculty of being able to drop off, or awaken, almost at will. He sleeps lightly, not because he is afraid of being robbed—he never has enough money to worry about that—but because he is very cautious about oversleeping. The vagrant who is still sleeping soundly when the train reaches the end of the line is more than likely to be picked up and lodged in jail by the transportation police.

Upon reaching the end of the line, Shelby walks up the stairs from the train platform to the next level. The turnstiles are at this level, and rest rooms have been placed inside the turnstiles. He retires to one of these rest rooms, finds a booth, fastens the door, and smokes a leisurely cigarette. It is supposedly a misdemeanor to carry lighted tobacco within the turnstile area, but Shelby says he discovered quite early in his career that even the police use the privacy of the rest rooms to have a quiet cigarette. Of course, he takes no chances. If there is a policeman anywhere on the turnstile level, he will forgo his smoke.

After his cigarette, he goes back to the train platform and boards the next train going in the opposite direction from the one he has just come. He quickly settles into a seat and goes to sleep again. He remains asleep until he reaches the other end of the line, then, as before, has his smoke and reboards a train. This time his nap is much shorter because he debarks at the Jay Street-Borough Hall station in Brooklyn and transfers to the Sixth Avenue subway. On this he makes a full round trip, going all the way out to Queens, back to the Brooklyn end of the line, and then back to Jay Street. There he reboards the Eighth Avenue, which he rides back to Penn Station.

The whole trip consumes from four and a half to five and a half hours, during the course of which he has probably netted four hours of sleep. Over the months he has learned many of the habits and assignments of the transportation police, and he tries to keep himself from being too familiar a figure. For this reason he does not depend entirely upon the subway and does not dare ride it oftener than every other night.

On his off nights, in good weather, he sometimes uses the two great parks, Central and Prospect. By varying his hours of repose, carefully selecting secluded spots, and transferring his resting places often, he can spend one night a week in either one or the other of them. Also, in warm weather, there are fire escapes. Because he knows the city as well as he does, Shelby has been able to locate several covered, and therefore secluded ones. Most of them are attached to theaters or warehouses and offer ideal accommodations. For some reason, the police never seem to bother vagrants who occupy these emergency exits. And on three or four occasions during the summer Shelby manages to get out to one of the beaches near the city. He can sleep unmolested there, especially on a hot night. There are always legitimate sleepers, as he calls them, who are trying to escape the heat.

Naturally, in the fall, winter, and early spring, Shelby has to find other places. The benches in the waiting rooms at Grand Central, Penn Station, and the Port Authority Bus Terminal are his favorites outside of the subway. As in every other place, however, there are strict rules of conduct which must be observed. Shelby learned early that the station police in each of the three establishments have set habits. They make two routine checks during the course of a night. At Grand Central, for example, these checks come at one-thirty and five-thirty. Between the checks there are both policemen and plain-clothes men on duty in the waiting room throughout the night, and they wander up and down, carefully checking trouble spots. Ordinarily, however, these roving guardians will not disturb people who are stretched out on the benches asleep. Between the checks, therefore, it is possible to get almost four hours of uninterrupted sleep in a supine position. Conditions at Penn Station are about the same, and at the Bus Terminal the checks are farther apart, but the lights are brighter and the crowds larger, giving less room to stretch out.

Shelby keeps, as part of his equipment for sleeping in one of the three terminals, three tickets: to Poughkeepsie, New York; Princeton, New Jersey; and Elizabeth, New Jersey, one for each of the three lines. Inspection of time-tables has revealed that there are no busses or trains leaving New York for these points between one and six in the morning. In emergencies, should the station police question him too closely, Shelby flashes the appropriate ticket and claims that he missed the last train and is waiting for the first one in the morning. This has always worked, but on one occasion a station policeman escorted him to a six-

thirty train and made certain he got on it. Shelby got off at
125th Street and walked back to Grand Central.

Shelby regards sleeping in hotel lobbies as an unsatisfactory experience, yet he feels bound to try it every now
and then. No lobby can be occupied during the night, and
daytime occupancy is limited to about two hours at most.
While house officers will not ordinarily run a respectably
dressed man out into the street, they will shake him awake
every hour or so. In order to get four hours of sleep,
Shelby estimates that he has to visit eight hotels during a
day. He always apologizes profusely for having dozed off
and never visits the same hotel oftener than every third
month.

Shelby says that it is always advisable to carry something
when sleeping in a lobby. House officers are apt to respect
a man's privacy if he has an umbrella or brief case lying
in his lap. When Shelby plans to use a hotel lobby, he will
wander up and down the subway trains the day before
until he finds what he is looking for. Subways are full of
things that are suitable for hotel lobbies. He always turns in
whatever he has found to the Transit Authority's Lost and
Found Department after he has used it, and he is always
careful to check back later to find out whether there has
been any reward. He collected $12.50 this way last year.

Shelby thinks that all-night theaters are the most overrated sleeping places for men like himself. He has used
them, and still does occasionally, but compared to the subway, they are inordinately expensive and their seats, though
much softer, are much less suited to sleeping. They tip
back too much, and the head is apt to snap backward instead of forward. This always awakens Shelby. Furthermore, one cannot very well lean one's head on one's arm
when elbow resting room has to be fought for with one's
neighbor. The pictures are noisy in unexpected places, and
the sounds that are thrown out from the screen are loud and
unorthodox. On top of this, Shelby has found that no
matter what picture is being shown, he cannot keep from
watching it to see how it comes out. Thus, instead of
getting some sleep, he gets entertained.

Most people do their personal grooming in the privacy of
their own homes. Because Henry Shelby is homeless, he
cannot. But for two reasons he places more importance on
his personal appearance than he does on having a place to

sleep. First, he is naturally a neat and tidy man to whom un-
cleanliness is distasteful. Second, good grooming is a safety
factor in his existence. The police will always pick up an
unkempt man and will generally walk right by a tidy man.
A shower is not only a comfort, but a good investment.

From each five-dollar bill he gets, Shelby sets aside
enough money to provide himself with a bath. If he goes
six days without one, he will stop eating until he can pay
for one. Most of Shelby's baths are taken in the public
rooms of Grand Central Station and cost sixty-five cents.
Shaving is also a problem. At Shelby's age, he cannot go
for more than twenty-four hours without acquiring a
heavily shaded face. After that his beard is apt to become
a heavy stubble. Nervertheless, he tries to stretch the time
between shaves to at least thirty-six hours for economic
reasons: it costs twenty-five cents to use one of the booths
at Grand Central set aside for this purpose. Like most New
York City vagrants, Shelby always carries a safety razor in
his pocket and will take any opportunity he can to get in
a quick, free shave and a chance to brush his teeth. He
uses ordinary soap for shaving cream.

Clothing is another important item of appearance. With
the exception of his outer garments, Shelby owns two of
everything: two white shirts, two suits of underwear, two
pairs of socks, and two neckties. One set is always on his
back and the other is usually in storage at some laundry in
the Grand Central area. Whenever he takes his bath, Shelby
drops by the laundry first and picks up his clean linen.
After his shower he carefully wraps the soiled clothes in a
bundle and leaves them in another laundry to be washed.

His outer garments are kept as neat as possible. Once or
twice a week he drops in at one of the small tailor shops
around town and sits in his shirttail while his coat and
trousers are being pressed. Unfortunately, he has never
found a place where he can sit in a booth while the clothes
are being cleaned. When his garments are quite dirty, and
he gets enough money ahead, he picks up his clean laundry
and retires to a cheap but good hotel. There he engages
a room, paying for it in advance. Once the door is closed
on the bellhop, he strips and calls valet service. For the
next twenty-four hours, while the cleaners are at work on
his coat and trousers, he spends his time in bed, or under
the shower. He has slept for twenty-two hours on these

occasions, and taken as many as fifteen showers. He never gets too much sleep or too many showers.

The whole twenty-four-hour period in the hotel, including cleaning, costs him about seven dollars. Shelby considers this gross extravagance, since his weekly average expenditure is about eight dollars, but for some time he never seemed to accumulate enough money to buy a second suit. Besides, he always comes out of his stay with a tremendous sense of pleasure and well-being.

One of the astounding things about Shelby's existence is that he has become a recluse, just as surely as though he lived on a desert island. For three or four days at a time he will speak to no one, nor will anyone speak to him. He is not solitary by nature, but his way of life and his desire to continue it without molestation impose this penalty upon him. While he might like to engage the policeman in the Grand Central waiting room in conversation, he realizes that if he did, he might be recognized easily the next time he visited there, and all subsequent visits would gradually peg him as a homeless person, making him liable to arrest and harassment.

This solitude has brought him one great problem which he senses but finds difficult to describe: the problem of passage of time. Shelby is waiting for something. He himself does not know what it is. When it comes he will either go back into the world from which he came or sink out of sight in the morass of alcoholism or despair that has engulfed other vagrants. While he is waiting, he is plagued by a restlessness that keeps him on the move for seventeen or eighteen hours a day. He is likely to say that he moves about as much as he does because policemen will not stop a man who looks as though he is coming from some place or going to some place. What he does not say, because he does not realize it, is that he is working to keep his time occupied.

Shelby's search for entertainment has led him into every nook and cranny of the city and brought him knowledge that he might not otherwise have gained. One idiosyncrasy that he has discovered but cannot account for is the attitude of station policemen toward book readers. After seven-thirty in the evening, in order to read a book in Grand Central or Penn Station, a person either has to wear horn-rimmed glasses or look exceptionally prosperous. Anyone else is apt to come under surveillance. On the other hand, newspaper readers never seem to attract attention and even the seediest vagrant can sit in Grand Central all night without being molested if he continues to read a paper. Shelby therefore spends one or two hours a night going over the daily papers. He regularly reads all seven final editions of New York journals, which he picks out of trash baskets.

Shelby is extraordinarily fond of museums and galleries and has become something of an art expert. Vagrants are rarely molested in New York museums and galleries. Shelby is apt to smile and say this is because the guards can never distinguish between a legitimate bum and an artistic one. They never disturb a person like him because they never know when they are trying to eject an artist who is holding a one-man show on the third floor.

Shelby began frequenting the big marble-coated buildings many months ago in search of shelter and warmth. He followed the guides around on their tours, often three or four times a day. In order to seem part of the group making the tour he would ask questions. And by this time he knows enough to stump most of the guides. He has developed a genuine love for the subject, knows where every show in town is being held and what it contains, and is thinking of trying to do a little painting himself. But when he goes to the shows he is also still on the lookout for some obscure nook or cranny where he can stretch out and sleep for an hour or two. Even a corner behind a Grecian column where a man can sleep upright without interruption is valuable.

Another of Shelby's pastimes is to take the ferry ride from the Battery to Staten Island and back. He calls this the poor man's ocean voyage. Unfortunately, the round trip costs ten cents, which puts it in the luxury class. More often, he boards one of the numerous Central Railroad of New Jersey ferries and makes three or four round trips to the Jersey shore. If he gets on during the rush-hour periods, he is not noticed and there is no expense.

Pursuing this pastime Shelby has picked up a surprising amount of information on navigation, and he is rapidly becoming an authority on the New York tidal flow. He seems to get a great deal of enjoyment out of criticizing the pilots of the ferries if they do not bring their vessels squarely into the slips, and almost the first thing he reads in the New York papers is the shipping news. Two or three times a week he journeys to the waterfront to watch the arrival or departure of one of the big liners. On other occasions he will go down to the Jersey ferry slips and board the little vessel that he estimates will come closest to the big ships as they move up the river or put out to sea.

The city offers other free sources of diversion, too. Shelby always follows a fire engine; has a nose for street fights; and, if he stumbles upon an accident, never leaves the scene until the last policeman has closed his notebook. He stops to listen to every sidewalk preacher he comes across and likes to sing the hymns just for the pleasure of singing something. He knows every major construction project in town, but rarely watches such routine phases of the work as excavation or riveting. He looks the site over and then shows up at the exact moment some critical problem is about to be solved.

He is a steady visitor at the various courts around town, and is what he describes as a sucker for band music. For this reason, he believes he is happier in New York than he would be in any other city in the world. New York is the only place where there is a parade of some kind every day in the year. On some days there are two or three. Last Armistice Day, Shelby visited five parades and took part in one.

The peculiar advantages of the microfilm room of the New York Public Library, which he came upon almost by accident, are probably Shelby's unique discovery. He had been advised by another vagrant that the library was a good place to keep warm on a cold day, and that it offered an opportunity for an hour or two of sleep. Several days later he made his first call there, provided with what he considered a plausible excuse for visiting the institution. He went to the main desk and asked for a copy of the New York *Times* for November 10, 1936. He was referred to the microfilm room, where the attendant produced a roll of film instead of the paper. He was then escorted to one of several viewing machines which were placed helter-skelter in a sort of alcove off to one side of a large room. Shelby put the film in the machine and looked at the image. Within half an hour, as he turned the crank, he dozed off. He was not disturbed and eventually woke up about five hours later.

He says now that at the time this seemed too good to be true, so a week later he went back again to see if it was an accident. He arrived about nine-fifteen in the morning and slept until almost four-thirty in the afternoon, again without being disturbed.

He since has become cognizant of several things. Most men in his condition who visit the Public Library go to the reading rooms. Either they have never heard of the microfilm room or they underestimate its possibilities. Consequently, the attendants there have never met a real vagrant face to face. They assume that anyone who has heard of microfilm and wishes to use it is in search of learning. They check the film out to the applicant and never follow up. Moreover, the accommodations are very comfortable. The room is warm, and the upright film-display stands give a man an excellent place to rest his head.

For some time, Shelby put the microfilm room at the top of his list as a place of shelter, then suddenly he realized that it was a far more valuable place for pure entertainment. He never goes there to sleep now, but he often goes in early in the morning and spends the entire day reading. He has read all the old issues of the New York *Times* that are available on film, all his favorite comic strips from the date of their inception to the present, and every column Damon Runyon ever wrote.

A by-product of his many hours in the microfilm room is a system for playing the races which he developed by virtue of having been able to study every racing chart published in New York over the past twenty years. He has put this system to a test twice. At one time he worked quite steadily for almost a month and, with $25 in his pocket, visited Aqueduct Race Track, where he won $87.40, after expenses. Prudently, he took the money and bought himself a new suit of clothes, leaving the original $25 untouched. A few days later he took the money and went to Belmont Park, where he lost it all. He hasn't visited the track since, but he remains an avid racing fan and plays the horses regularly in the microfilm room. Nowadays, however, he saves all the races until cold weather sets in and plays during the winter months. He never looks at the racing results beforehand. "I might just as well be honest about it," he says.

Shelby's favorite of all forms of recreation is walking.

He usually walks the streets of Manhattan for four to ten hours a day, covering anywhere from five to twenty-five miles. He has walked the full length of every up and down avenue in the city and crossed the island on every crosstown street. He is a walking encyclopedia on plaques, and knows every traffic bottleneck and short cut in town. He loves to window-shop and knows when most of the stores change their displays. At some time every day he manages to pass the window of the Christian Science Reading Room on Park Avenue and solemnly reads the Bible passage marked there.

At one time he estimated that he had about exhausted the possibilities of exploration in Manhattan and decided to concentrate on Brooklyn. He crossed the Brooklyn Bridge on foot one day, and on two other occasions took the subway. At the end of the third trip he gave the project up. "Walking in Brooklyn is like walking in Lansing, Michigan. I have the feeling I've seen everything before," he says. "Manhattan isn't like that."

At present, Henry Shelby seems content to take things as they come. "I don't know how long I'll live this life," he told me not long ago, as he traced a design in the dirt with his foot. "I don't have much trouble. I've never gotten drunk and lain in a doorway all day. My name's never been on a police blotter for vagrancy. I haven't had to beg. Maybe if things were like they were twenty years ago, when everybody was a bum, I might change. Maybe something will happen that will force me to change, one way or another. Yes, I guess that's about it, but it hasn't happened yet, and things seem so easy and natural this way, the way they are now, that it's just as though it was supposed to be that way. I'm just not going to look at the future. All I can tell anybody, now, is that I intend to be up at a little delicatessen I know on Broadway. They serve a hell of a good boiled beef dinner up there for sixty-eight cents." He looked up at one of the big street clocks. "Which reminds me. If I'm going to get there by six o'clock, I'd better get going. Takes me almost an hour to walk it." I asked him why he didn't take the subway.

"Subways are for sleeping," Shelby said, smiled, and walked off.

The Man Who Can Do Anything

Mitts Flanagan is a man who can do anything. No dream seems impossible of achievement. Nothing seems too difficult. A few years ago he was sitting at the bar of a place in the East Fifties when a stranger walked in and took the next stool. The stranger got to talking and mentioned the fact that he had just come from a piano recital at Town Hall. Mitts held up those big hands of his and looked at them with a martyred expression.

"I could have been a piano player," he said, "a good one, too. If I'd only listened to my mother when I was a kid, I might have been playing the piano tonight in Town Hall myself."

For most people, drunk or sober, that probably would have been the end of the whole business, but Flanagan sat at the bar until it closed, thinking how frustrated he was. After he'd been put out into the street, he wandered down Lexington Avenue, all the way to Gramercy Park, scuffing along like a kid, his hands in his pockets, whistling the tunes he would have been playing if he'd taken his mother's advice. When dawn came, he was still walking. Flanagan is no Walter Mitty. He entered the first drug store he found open, went back to the phone booths, and started copying down the names and addresses of piano teachers from the Yellow Pages. By noon that day he had taken his first lesson. By seven o'clock that evening, he had taken two more, each one from a different teacher. He was then very tired with the lessons and with the drinks between lessons, so he went back to his hotel to bed. A night's sleep did not deter him from his purpose. He was back at the lessons again as soon as he woke up. He took piano lessons for twelve straight days, between drinks. Toward the end of the second week he was much too tired to sit on the piano bench, so he conceived the idea of getting a substitute. He walked down to the 14th Street automat, which is the same to Third Avenue as Toots Shor's is to Broadway, and asked the bums who hang out in the neighborhood if any of them were frustrated piano players. Flanagan is well known in that part of town, and he had no trouble in recruiting a quartet of interested people. It was late at night, however, and Mitts never got any of them to a piano. They spent the night in various bars discussing music, and while they were on the way to a teacher's studio the next morning, Flanagan lost them all in doorways along the route of advance. On the way up Third Avenue, however, he noticed the children playing on the sidewalk, and this gave him an even better idea. By evening, he had the names of six or seven children who wanted nothing more than to play the piano. After a little more sleep he rounded up the candidates and marched them to the nearest piano teacher for aptitude tests. In this fashion he narrowed the field down to two boys. He took these two home and got their mothers' permission to take regular lessons. He bought two secondhand upright pianos and had them delivered to the homes. For the next three weeks he was at the piano teacher's faithfully whenever it was time for one of the boys to take a lesson, solemnly nodding his head and keeping time with his feet. By the end of that period, the binge had about run its course and Flanagan quietly disappeared into a sanitarium. Afterwards, when he was sober, he had forgotten all about it, who the children were, and who the teacher was. And he couldn't play chopsticks himself.

New Yorkers who have come to know Mitts Flanagan over a period of twenty-five years realize that he is a wealthy man and that he made his fortune as a businessman. He is a huge man, standing well over six feet, and he weighs nearly 250 pounds, very little of it fat. He has an open, good-natured face and wears rimless spectacles. When he is sober he is carefree and laughs often with a loud, booming sound. When he has been drinking, he is solemn and stern faced, pursuing the subject at hand with an august majesty of purpose.

I have known Mitts Flanagan intimately for many years

myself and I know that he lives in Boston, Massachusetts, where he is apparently well thought of. This is probably because he has never done his serious drinking there. Whenever he feels the weakness coming upon him, he gets to New York as fast as he can and lives out his binge in the world of flophouses and all-night bars that fringe the brighter and more inviting parts of the city. Mitts Flanagan's binges may come five days or five years apart. In between he never takes a drink. A binge may last anywhere from two weeks to two months.

Very few people in New York know Flanagan's real name. Everyone takes it for granted that the Mitts Flanagan is a pseudonym, which, indeed, it is. He is married, but has no children, and his wife has long since come to accept the periods when he disappears. There is never any question about Flanagan's faithfulness. Because of his obvious love for his wife, no one in New York asks him about her any more. An inquiry would invariably set him off on the most prolonged song fest in town. He has probably driven more people out of bars with his loud, baritone rendition of "Jeannie with the Light Brown Hair" than anyone in history. The mere mention of her will bring a tender, almost beatific, smile to his face, but it never drives him home. It just sends him in search of music.

Flanagan's wife probably puts up with his vagaries for the same reason that everyone else does—his essential good will. He wants the admiration of anyone he meets and will bend every effort to acquire it. In doing so, he usually tries to identify himself intimately with the subject dearest to his listener's heart. If he happens to run into a geographer when he is drinking, he is quite likely to cast out the information that he once accompanied Admiral Byrd to the South Pole. If he talks to a city fireman, he is invariably reminded of his own days on the rear end of a hook and ladder truck. In his time, by his own account, he has been a singer, yachtsman, writer, mountain climber, steeple jack, big game hunter, little game hunter, actor, chef, professional dancer, bartender, cardsharp, and detective. He is apt to add to this list at almost any time, and he will demonstrate if the means are at hand.

The one subject that Mitts Flanagan likes most to talk about is his college career at St. Bonaventure. I have kept track of this glorious chapter from the past in a methodical manner as it has unfolded over the years. I found that Flanagan played guard, tackle, and end on the football team, captained it in his senior year, and was St. Bonaventure's only three-time All-American. He was center and captain on the basketball team. He was captain and catcher on the baseball team. He was shot-putter on the track team. He was captain and intercollegiate champion on the golf team, and the only man in college who ever shot two holes-in-one during one single round. He was captain and light-heavyweight on the boxing team, and, as a matter of fact, earned his way through college by boxing professionally under an assumed name. He was also stroke on the crew. (St. Bonaventure has no crew.) Flanagan was so good at these various sports in college that he went on, afterwards, to play tackle for the Green Bay Packers, put the shot on the 1924 Olympic team, catch for Syracuse in the International League, and play goalie for the Detroit Red Wings. It was a remarkable career, one must admit, and Mitts has filled twenty-two scrapbooks with pictures to commemorate it. Every now and then, as I thumb through the pages, I see Flanagan's beaming face smiling out from under a football helmet, or his big bulk poised with the discus ready to fly out into space. The largest number of pictures, however, are action shots, taken at a moment when Mitts has his back turned. He is shooting a basket, or blocking home plate in the middle of a cloud of dust which has improvidently obscured his features. Now and then he brings a handful of gold footballs to New York, or a suitcase full of loving cups with his name engraved upon them. On several occasions he has appeared in one bar or another wearing a St. Bonaventure letter sweater, and he once put in a courtesy appearance at the Olympic Trials on Long Island, clad in his own official white Olympic sweater. At least it had his name sewed on the bottom.

Flanagan does not always confine himself to talking about his exploits. He often becomes a man of action in a determined effort to prove that he has not yet lost all of his skill. In the summer of 1952, the United States Open Golf Tournament was played at a nearby New Jersey course. Mitts had arrived in New York late in the evening of the final day of the tournament and had settled down at a bar in the East Forties to drink. This bar was regularly patron-ized by newsmen from the *Daily News* and *Mirror*. Shortly after one in the morning, two sportswriters came in. They had evidently just finished writing their stories about the championship and were sitting next to Flanagan, discussing some aspect of the play. If any conversation lasts long enough, Flanagan will always become involved in it, and, on this occasion he asked a few questions, received a few answers, and bought a few drinks. For over an hour the three men talked in a friendly manner about golf and great golfers. Towards the end of the conversation, Flanagan sighed, somewhat soulfully, let a tear appear in his eye, and dropped the information that he had wasted his life. He told about having been captain of the St. Bonaventure golf team in his undergraduate days, and described the finals of the intercollegiate tournament in which he had been defeated on the sixty-third hole of a play-off.

"If I'd only listened to Bobby Jones," Flanagan said, "I might have been in that final out there today. He wanted me to play professional golf, but I didn't know enough to listen to him."

"It wouldn't take you long to recapture your skill," one of the sportswriters said. "It's something you don't lose. You only get rusty. Why don't you play a little? You might find you're not so bad."

"Do you really think so?" Flanagan asked him.

"Sure."

Flanagan thought a minute.

"Aw," he said. "I'm too old."

"Gene Sarazen plays every year and he's in his fifties," the sportswriter said.

When the sportswriters left the bar, they patted Flanagan on the back and told him to keep his chin up. By the time he followed them out into the street, two or three hours later, his eyes were shining. He'd seen some kind of a vision. It had to do with an unheralded, unknown golfer who came from nowhere, dropping approach shots into the cup from 300 yards out, to win the next National Open. While carefully perusing the morning papers he noted that the Westchester Open Golf Tournament was to be held within a few weeks, and determined that he would begin his comeback there. The next morning, when the stores opened, he was standing in front of a sporting goods shop, waiting to get in and buy a set of golf clubs. With these in

hand he made his way to a public course on Long Island
and went to work. He played thirty-six holes the first day.
They were terrible. The next morning, his jaw set in a
grim line, he returned, accompanied by a caddy he had
hired in a Columbus Avenue bar, and played another
thirty-six holes. His game had not improved. On the third
morning he began taking lessons, but it didn't help. When,
at the end of a week, he hadn't done any better, he deemed
it time to step up his practice. He began arriving at the
golf course at dawn every morning and worked on the
practice putting green until someone came along to dis-
possess him. Then he would begin his thirty-six hole stint
in an electric golf cart driven by his Columbus Avenue
caddy. Attached to the dashboard of the vehicle was a
cocktail shaker, and in the golf bag were ample ingredients
for mixing Daiquiris. The caddy had his own supply of
whiskey. By the end of each round, Flanagan would be
operating unsteadily, and the caddy would scarcely be
navigating at all. The high point of this particular part of
the training grind came towards the end of the second week
when the caddy was arrested for drunken driving while
trying to cross the highway from one nine-hole layout to
another. Once the daily thirty-six hole round was finished,
Flanagan would start out in a taxicab to visit all the practice driving ranges he could find. He would not desist, usually, until the last floodlighted one was closed for the night,
and even then he was apt to stop on the way back into
town and pick up a few holes on a miniature golf course if
he happened to pass one.

Unfortunately, Flanagan's game never seemed to improve and as the deadline for the Westchester Open approached, it became apparent that desperate measures
would have to be taken. One night, after exhausting the
supply of practice driving ranges, Mitts retired to an
Eleventh Avenue bar where he began lamenting the lack
of further practice facilities. One of his friends who was
in a slightly more inebriated condition than he was, suggested that Flanagan step outside and take a look at Eleventh Avenue. It was then three o'clock in the morning, and
the traffic was almost non-existent. It seemed like an entirely reasonable place to drive golf balls and that is exactly
what Mitts did, standing calmly, almost majestically, at the
corner of 59th Street by the IRT power station, and teeing

off in the general direction of the Lincoln Tunnel. He had optimistically dispatched bar patrons as far south as 45th Street to intercept traffic and keep it from running into golf balls. Other patrons were stationed at intervals up and down the Avenue to retrieve the balls. Unhappily, Flanagan had developed a bad slice and, before the police arrived on the scene, he had broken $250 worth of windows. He was arrested on a drunk charge and booked on several counts of disturbing the peace and suspicion of malicious destruction of property. He was out of jail by noon the next day, however, after paying a fine of $50 and agreeing to replace the broken windows. He headed straight for the golf course to resume his practice.

Upon returning to the bar that night, he was greeted by his friends, some of whom he had bailed out of jail a few hours before. There ensued a good deal of reminiscing about the sight of golf balls bouncing off buildings in the middle of the night. It seemed, in retrospect, like a rather hilarious experience to some of the men, but Flanagan got prouder every time someone compared one of his drives to a bullet. One of the men at the bar made the fatal mistake of asking Mitts how he was able to get so much power in his drives. Flanagan, solemn and professorial, proceeded to demonstrate, but in order to keep from angering the police and the residents of Eleventh Avenue, he demonstrated inside the bar, standing at the back of the room and driving the balls in the general direction of the waterfront, hitting them off the tee as fast as one of the eager spectators could set them up. Before the bartender was able to crawl along behind the bar on his hands and knees and make his escape out the side door to the nearest police call box, the saloon was a shambles. Flanagan had overcompensated for his slice, and the result was a bad hook. It effectively swept all the glasses and whiskey bottles from in front of the mirror. The mirror itself was not broken, but everything else was, including the two plate glass windows at the front. The police magistrate sentenced Flanagan to thirty days in jail for this episode. By the time he was released, he was sober and the Westchester Open was over. He gave his golf clubs to one of the inmates at the jail and forgot the whole thing.

Mitts Flanagan likes to take part in anything, and he does not confine his activities to the more popular, organized types of competition. Whenever he comes across a group of boys playing stick ball in an empty parking lot, or that peculiar combination of handball and baseball that they play by bouncing the ball off buildings, he always gets right into the game, playing it as though his life depended upon it and joining in the arguments as though they were the most important thing in the world. The boys do not resent his butting in because he never condescends in his dealings with them. He creates the illusion that he has raised the game to an adult level. It is as though Babe Ruth had come to join them. On one occasion he came across a baseball game that had been interrupted by a free-for-all fight among the players. He stopped the fight, not to lecture about the virtue of peace, but to complain that the boys were not fighting right. Before he was finished, he had launched into a tale of his own ring experiences. The boys seemed so impressed that Flanagan got on a train that evening and journeyed all the way to Boston to get the scrapbooks he had compiled on his boxing exploits. For good measure, he brought along two or three championship belts he had acquired, and a whole box of miniature golden gloves which he passed out at the end of his next lecture. Although Flanagan's scrapbooks have been treated by some adults as a big joke, they were not a joke to the boys who spent hours poring over them.

Flanagan is genuinely fond of children of any age. On a hot afternoon in summer, he will sit on the front steps of a brownstone house for hours with ten or twelve of the smaller ones gathered about him, listening to his stories. He is a great storyteller and mixes up the old classics like the "Three Bears" and "Red Riding Hood" with new ones that he invents as he goes along. On at least one occasion, his affection for small children got Mitts involved in a project that almost overcame him. He was walking along Second Avenue one day when he became engaged in a conversation with a little girl. She spoke rather forlornly of wanting a dachshund. This was too much for Flanagan, so he took her by the hand and bought her one. Afterwards, he got to thinking about it, and it seemed a shame to him that so many children in New York were without dogs. During a discussion with some of his friends in a bar, someone suggested that there ought to be a foundation set up for furnishing dogs to poor children. It developed that dogs—rather than fresh air and summer camps—were what the children really wanted. By morning of the next day, Flanagan had had a good opportunity to think this out to its logical conclusion. There wasn't a man in the United States better equipped than he to undertake such a project. By ten o'clock he had already purchased six animals of varying breeds. Next he hired a bum he knew to take over some of the leashes. When his assistant knew what was afoot, he suggested that Flanagan wouldn't have enough money to go around buying pedigreed dogs. Inasmuch as children did not usually know one make of dog from another, it might be better if they just passed the word along the grapevine for all the bums to bring in any stray dogs they found. This seemed sensible. Toward the end of the week, Flanagan was trailed around by ten or twelve assistants and about forty dogs. It was at this time that he decided the animals were tired and needed a place to sleep. He finally located a vacant building on Avenue B and paid a month's rent. As soon as he moved in with them, the dogs started barking, fighting, whining, howling, and playing tag. Flanagan sent out and bought a big easy chair and sat in it in the middle of the room, trying to keep the dogs quiet. He sang to them, he told them all his stories, he whistled, petted them, lectured to them, and spanked them. In the meantime, in order to keep the place clean, he had to hire sweepers, shovelers, and dog walkers. New dogs kept coming in all the time until the foundation had a hundred or so animals on its hands. It did not seem to occur to Flanagan that it was time to start getting rid of the dogs, and it might not have occurred to him at all if some of the neighbors hadn't objected. By that time he himself was not in any shape to undertake the problem of giving the dogs away, so he delegated it to a committee of his assistants which he dubbed the Board of Directors of the Foundation. These men began a door-to-door canvass, each with a dog. Nobody was having any. Since new dogs kept coming in and none were going out, even Flanagan became a little desperate. He sent out a general alarm, and for a week or two a visitor in New York could easily have gotten the impression that every bum in the city had a dog on a leash. The whole episode ended when one of the dogs took an intense dislike to his benefactor. After growling every time Flanagan took a drink for two or three days, the dog finally bit him. After that, he nipped Mitts every time the bottle was lifted.

"He must've come from a broken home," Flanagan complained to me.

The problem of the biting dog became a matter of general discussion along 14th Street until one of the bums happened to think that the animal might be mad. At that point Flanagan was rushed off to the nearest hospital for observation. Luckily, the animal wasn't rabid, so the only effect the biting had in the end was to sober Mitts up. Long before he was out of the hospital, most of the dogs had been carted off to the pound.

The thoughtfulness shown in rushing Flanagan off to a hospital typifies the regard that New York bums hold for him. He is just as fond of them. In the years that he has been visiting the city on his drinking bouts, he has done a great many things for which he is remembered. He has advanced medical expenses for scores of down-and-outers, and he has paid the funeral expenses of many of his friends who would otherwise have been consigned to graves in potter's field. While most of the vagrants are appreciative of this type of thing, they are even more grateful for the fact that Flanagan's charity extends far beyond some of the more orthodox outlets. He never enters a bar in the more run-down areas of the city without buying at least one round of drinks for the whole house. He never turns down a man's request for a quarter or a half-dollar, even when he knows that the money will be spent for liquor.

"Some guys will be helped more by a drink than they will by a meal or a bed," he once told me.

He always comes to New York with a pocketful of traveler's checks, and he rarely leaves with any. It is an unofficial custom among the bums to keep an eye on Mitts. There is usually someone close at hand so that no crook will try to roll him and take the money away.

By far the biggest share of his money goes for wages. In practically all of his projects, he needs help, as witness the dog foundation. His standard rate is $10 a day, plus adequate liquid refreshments to get a man from one duty to the next. It is a generous arrangement, but even if it were a dollar a day, most of the bums would work for him because any job he thinks up is usually good for a lot of laughs.

On one of his visits to New York, shortly after World

War II, Flanagan checked in at a Lexington Avenue hotel. Towards the end of his first day, as he was riding up to his room, the elevator became stuck between floors. Mitts was alone in the car with the operator at the time and during the half hour which ensued while they waited for rescue, they talked. The operator explained what had to be done to raise the car, and the principles of modern elevator operation. Flanagan went to bed thinking about elevators. The next morning, when he awoke, he attacked the problem with some intensity. He got the want-ad sections from all the morning papers and set out to apply for every job in town where an elevator operator was needed. The longer he walked and the more he was rebuffed, the more indignant he became. At the end of a week, he walked into a Third Avenue establishment and banged his fist on the bar.

"By God," he said. "I'll buy my own damned elevator. Here I am, a man who took a course in hotel management at St. Bonaventure, and I can't even get a job running an elevator. I'll show them."

Some of the more sober heads pointed out to Flanagan that if he bought an elevator he'd probably have to buy a building to put it in, and that could be a pretty expensive proposition. One of the less sober ones then suggested that it might be a good idea if Flanagan *rented* an elevator. The more he had to drink, the more sensible this idea seemed, and he ended up by dispatching three or four scouts to find him one.

"And none of your God damned push-button ones, either," he is reputed to have said. "I want one with levers. Those damned buttons are no challenge at all."

The elevator of Flanagan's dreams was finally located in a twelve-story loft building on West 34th Street. It was an old-fashioned, cage-type elevator in an open shaft. The building superintendent presented some difficulty, laughing when renting it was suggested, but one of the scouts discovered that the night watchman was more vulnerable. He was addicted to bourbon whiskey. After several pints were applied, and after a hundred dollar bill was produced, arrangements were made. Flanagan would be allowed to run the elevator all he wanted to between the hours of midnight and four in the morning. He spent two days getting ready. He went to a tailor and had a bright blue operator's uniform custom-made for him. He also spent several hours practicing the proper demeanor for elevator operators in front of a mirror in his hotel room. Then he went down to several of his favorite bars on Third Avenue and hired twenty-four men. At midnight that night he ushered them all into the building and stationed them on different floors, each supplied adequately with liquid refreshments, of course. After that he went to work. The men would push the buzzer and Flanagan would pick them up and carry them back and forth between floors. This continued for five full nights with Flanagan standing stone-faced, proper, and businesslike at the controls of his car, ferrying the twenty-four bums on their imaginary errands. It might have gone on indefinitely, or at least until Flanagan's money gave out, if some of the bums and the night watchman hadn't reached the saturation point in the consumption of whiskey. When two or three began putting up the windows on the top floor of the building and whistling at the girls in Herald Square, the police were attracted. Flanagan himself escaped apprehension. As the police rode up and down in the elevator, rounding up the bums, he stood icily correct and apparently sober at the controls, offering no comment and taking a neutral stand in the proceedings, his nattily pressed blue uniform a testimony to the fact that he was a helpless victim of circumstances, a prisoner, as it were, of the rowdies who had taken over the building. Not one of his paid help gave him away, and at the end of the raid one of the policemen even apologized for causing him so much trouble. The next morning he went down and bailed everybody out of jail, but he had to give up the elevator because the night watchman had been fired. Long before he found another elevator to rent, his binge had run its course.

It has been more than two years now since Mitts Flanagan has been seen in New York. This has been one of his longest periods of abstinence. About six weeks ago, some of his friends were sitting around the 14th Street automat, wondering what had become of him. They were worried and took up a collection to send one of their number to Boston to see if everything was all right. The messenger has not yet returned, but Flanagan's friends refuse to be discouraged. The man they sent is a defrocked Pullman conductor. Perhaps somewhere, somehow, Flanagan has rented a railroad.

No Fixed Address

The busiest man I know in New York is Charlie Knutsen. We became friends in 1953 while I was working for an air-conditioning firm on the West Side. Charlie took an interest in me although he was several years my junior. He advised me on how to save money, get free meals, and find jobs. We used to walk to work together in the morning and home again at night. As he talked I was more and more surprised. I thought that I knew a lot about living cheaply in a city myself, but after listening to Charlie I realized I was only an amateur. In Charlie, a farm boy from Iowa, I had met a professional.

Charlie lives in other people's apartments.

This breathless existence started about eleven years ago. At that time Charlie was living with a rather handsome young actor in an apartment in the West Seventies. The two had been in the Navy together during the war and had both decided to try to crack the artistic barriers. The actor was something of a ladies' man. Every week or so he would come to Charlie and ask that the apartment be vacated for the week end so that a love affair could be consummated. At the time, Charlie was friendly with a great many young singers, dancers, and writers. They were all hopeful, and most of them were broke a good part of the time. The code by which they lived was a simple one. It involved taking in any homeless strays, for they never knew when they themselves might be homeless and need shelter. They took Charlie in for varying periods. By the time his roommate got married and ousted Charlie permanently, he had become an accomplished guest. Some of the places in which he stayed were vacant, the owners having gone off for a few days on visits or business. It struck Charlie that if he knew enough people in New York, someone ought to be going out of town all the time. He purchased a notebook and began keeping a list of names and addresses. The list has grown regularly for years, but he stopped adding to it lately. He now keeps it at a level of about eighty, but it may vary up or down from time to time as Charlie adds a new and especially likely friend, or deletes one of the girls who has gotten married. He automatically crosses off a bride, reasoning that she will give up traveling, or, if she doesn't, that she will leave a husband at home.

Charlie Knutsen has become a nomad. In all the ten years since he wholeheartedly adopted the plan, his longest single span of residence has amounted to a little more than sixty days, a period that he spent in the abode of a chorus girl who was traveling around the country with General Motors' Motorama. His ordinary span of residence is about two weeks—the usual vacation with pay allotted most New York workers. There have been innumerable week-end stays, and any number of one night stands. Charlie prefers *not* to stay in a place if the owner is home. He likes the illusion of having his own apartment. For that reason, the list of people from whom he accepts hospitality is composed chiefly of persons who are engaged in business that requires a lot of travel. Most are in one branch or another of the theatrical profession; they are singers, dancers, actresses, sports announcers, a few itinerant writers, and at least one professional baseball player.

Charlie's decision to live in other people's apartments involves more than just keeping a list of possible places. He has to keep his name and his problem constantly before his prospective hosts. In many of the apartments of people on his list he has posted reminders in prominent places, giving the post-office box number or the phone number of a friend through whom he can be reached in case they go out of town. He sends postcards at regular intervals and calls by the phone at odd moments. He reads *Variety, Billboard,* and other theatrical publications religiously to keep track of casting news, bookings, and just plain comings and goings. It is no exaggeration to say that Charlie knows almost as much about the lives of the people on his list as they do.

A man who lives in other people's apartments and who bombards them with constant reminders of his existence could develop into a pest. This is not the case with Charlie.

To begin with, practically all of his friends were broke and struggling at one time in their careers. They are no strangers to a makeshift way of life, and they fully understand what he is trying to do and why he is doing it. But there are reasons why he is a good man to know. He is valuable to persons with pets. He knows and understands cats, dogs, parakeets, and hamsters, and ministers to them as though they were his own. If a pet owner goes out of town at a time when Charlie is already billeted, he knows that he can depend on his pet being cared for anyway. Charlie will take the time to go clear across town to feed or walk an animal, even though he is not living in the owner's apartment. This little gesture of thoughtfulness and others like it have been extended often enough over the years to soften any hostility that Charlie's persistence might tend to raise. Another of Charlie's assets is his ability as a handy man. The first seventeen years of his life were spent on a farm where he learned the fundamentals of trades like carpentry, plumbing, and painting. What he didn't already know, he has picked up since coming to New York, where he has held an unusually wide variety of jobs. He can reupholster a sofa or repair a television set. Many of the people on his list save their odd jobs until Charlie comes. He has done cabinet work, installed new shower heads, and puttied windows. Needless to say, he has lived in almost every type of apartment in New York, from a cold water walk-up to a Sutton Place penthouse.

Charlie's decision to live in other people's apartments, once it was made and adhered to, resulted in some rather startling innovations in his mode of life. There is the matter of possessions. Because he moves as often as he does, he has reduced life to its minimum essentials. This saves him from carrying things from place to place. If a thing will not fit into his one suitcase, he doesn't want it. He has one good suit of clothes, one good shirt, and one good necktie. He rarely wears them. For work he keeps two sports shirts, two rather frayed white shirts, and a small supply of underwear and socks. If he has to wear a necktie, he wears his best one, or borrows one from his host of the moment. He has a pair of pants that he presses every morning with whatever flatiron goes with the apartment he is living in, and a sports jacket with leather patches on the elbows. If his current residence has a shoe shine kit in it, he shines his one pair of shoes. If not, he rubs them on the back of his pants.

If Charlie stays in an apartment for any length of time, he will eat it right down to the bare shelves. There is always bound to be something left in any refrigerator or cupboard when the owner goes away. Charlie will start out by doing away with the more obvious things like orange juice, milk, butt ends of roasts, and eggs. Then he goes to work on the staples. At one apartment where he stayed, there was nothing much left after a few days but three bottles of olives. This didn't stop Charlie. He went to work every day, for almost a week, with olive sandwiches for lunch. He has been known to buy a few things to put in the kitchen, but he gets only enough to allow him to carry a sandwich to work and have a cup of coffee and a piece of toast for breakfast. There was a time, when he first began living his nomadic existence, that Charlie cooked his own dinners in the apartments, but the discovery that he could solve his shelter problems inexpensively led him to consider an application of his principles to other fields. Nowadays, one of his biggest preoccupations is getting invited out to dinner every night.

Charlie Knutsen is systematic. His success in always being able to find a vacant apartment was due to his attention to detail. The same system works for getting free meals. Charlie is not only invited to dinner each evening, but he has a long waiting list of people who *want* to invite him to dinner. He keeps an appointment book with a list of invitations for three weeks ahead. As with apartments, Charlie feels that meal invitations are a volume proposition. He keeps a notebook, as usual, full of prospective hosts. The list of names, addresses, and telephone numbers in this book is much more voluminous than the apartment list. It includes almost everyone with whom Charlie has a speaking acquaintance, and he keeps in touch with all of them. He is incessantly telephoning, sending post cards, reminding them that he is alive. He figures that if he keeps at this, some of the people are bound to invite him to dinner. So far he has been eminently right. What is more, he seems to have an unending string of new names to add to the list. He never goes anywhere without adding at least one. Cocktail parties, which he attends quite often, especially in the summer months, add quite a few new acquaintances, but the people he meets on the various jobs he holds are by far the largest group.

In ten years, Charlie Knutsen has worked at more than forty different jobs in the metropolitan area. He has worked for big companies and for small companies. He has worked by himself, and he has worked in offices where there may be a hundred people. He has worked in all the boroughs of the city, and in every section of Manhattan, plus a few of the suburbs. He has been an accountant, a typist, and an office clerk. He has worked as a gardener on a big estate in Yonkers, as a valet to a wealthy man, as a cook for a foreign consulate, and as a janitor in an office building. He has sold men's haberdashery in a department store, milk from a wagon, produce in a supermarket, and has read meters for Consolidated Edison. He has driven a sight-seeing bus, served as a messenger in the garment district, collected refuse on a Department of Sanitation truck, and composed ads for the classified section of a newspaper. He has been a bellhop in a well-known midtown hotel, a draftsman for a large engineering firm, a desk clerk in a flophouse, and a board man for the stock exchange. Everywhere he works he makes friends. He makes them deliberately and methodically. He collects information about people's sacroiliacs, maternal grandfathers, and favorite face soaps. He finds out about the carburetors on their automobiles, the hymnbooks in their churches, and the fillings in their teeth. Once he finds out, he puts the information in his notebook. If he happens to be working alone, as he was at the time he read meters, he makes friends with the customers rather than fellow workers. He knows filling station operators all over town because he used to stop and talk with them when he was peddling milk. Their names are in his notebook, too. Charlie's collection of small facts sometimes pays off startling dividends. He has been one of the few New Yorkers who has been able to secure tickets to "My Fair Lady"—or to major sports events—almost at will. This came about partly through a small scrap of information he picked up, partly through his assiduous cultivation of people, and partly because of his habit of doing everything on a volume basis. When he was working for an air conditioning firm a few years ago, he went to the Polo Grounds one day as the guest of a friend. He noted that the box just in front of where he was sitting had the name of the company for which he worked hung on a little tin plate from the top railing. The next day he began inquiring around his office to find out how a person went about using those tickets. He found out that the box was used by the sales department and maintained for customers who might be visiting in town. He found out, also, that when they weren't used by customers they were turned back for general sale, but that the company was happy to have employees buy them if they weren't used. While investigating this, Charlie found out that the company also had a standing order for tickets to hit shows, which were used for the same purpose and handled in the same way. The secret of getting them was simply in knowing the man who had charge of them. This was easy for Charlie. He didn't stop with his own company. He checked back to every other place he had ever worked and found out that he knew fifteen or twenty men who controlled tickets to one thing and another. He has never used this information for his own benefit, primarily because it requires spending money, but he might go to a cocktail party and overhear someone lamenting the fact that he couldn't get tickets to "My Fair Lady." By calling enough of his friends and not being particular as to which night the tickets were for, Charlie would be able to get them for his new acquaintance. This type of thing results in all kinds of new leads, of course. It puts names in notebooks, brings invitations, and even gives Charlie a different kind of resource that he may be able to use somewhere else in the future. Incidentally, Charlie will follow up a favor like this. He will check to see if the tickets were delivered on time, if he can be of any help in getting the people to the theater, and check, afterwards, to see if everything was satisfactory. By the time he is finished with an episode such as this, he is almost an Old Friend.

Charlie takes a rather cavalier attitude towards all of his jobs. He changes them often, and for reasons that have his friends muttering to themselves. I knew him when he was working for a firm on the lower West Side and he suddenly got an apartment in the upper East Eighties; he immediately quit his job and got one nearer to where he lived. He will quit his job if there is no bank at hand to cash his pay check during lunch hour, and he will quit an inside job when he suddenly feels the need for fresh air.

Charlie is a better than average worker. He has to be because on any given day he is quite likely to have only a minimum amount of time to devote to it. His personal items of business sometimes exert so much pressure that he has to do what he is paid for in two or three hours. This requires great efficiency. The fact that he has never been fired from a job speaks well for his record. It is also little short of amazing because Charlie will put demands on almost any firm that would require a lesser person to be discharged. Almost the first thing he does when he takes a new job is to look over the company's resources. The telephone system is the first thing he investigates, because the telephone is practically the lifeline on which his existence depends. On an average day he will make twenty or thirty calls to friends. To a casual observer, nothing of import may seem to be said in the conversation that takes place. Charlie may only pass the time of day, but it is all part of that constant system which he uses to bring in invitations. The ideal situation, of course, is for Charlie to have his own phone on his desk with a direct outside line, but it is a rare thing for such good fortune to come to him. Usually he has to go through a switchboard. This makes him an avid cultivator of switchboard operators. Through one subterfuge or another he always manages to get a direct line to the outside from his extension for part of every day. When he is working on an outside job, he makes surveys of all available free telephones. One reason he became so well acquainted with so many filling station operators was because he was using their telephones as he passed by them on his milk route or meter reading route. When phones are not available, Charlie has to fall back on two-cent postal cards for communication, or operate through a series of codes. During periods when he is forced to use pay telephones, he carefully instructs the people by post card on what to do. If someone drops him a line asking when he will arrive for dinner, he will drop a card right back, saying that he will call at exactly three o'clock on the day in question. They are not to pick the phone up when it rings. If it rings seven times, that means Charlie will arrive at seven o'clock. After the required number of

rings, Charlie will hang up and get his dime back. With
his older and more intimate friends, he has long established
codes which he uses most of the time.

After surveying the telephone facilities in his office,
Charlie investigates the company stationery room. The
most important items he wants are stamped two-cent post
cards. If these aren't available, he will settle for stamped
envelopes. If he can obtain neither, he will find some excuse
for getting a large supply of stamps from the person who
disburses them, or become good friends with the custodian
of the postage meter. If the postage is controlled by a tightfisted person, Charlie is quite likely to quit his job and get
another. He sends out an average of twenty-five post cards
a day. If he doesn't send cards, he will dispatch short notes.
He rarely says very much, but what he does say is important. He may say that he has just written to say hello. He
may ask if there have been any new developments in
Grandma's attempt to solve the tie-breaking puzzle. He
may tell someone that he's just found out where there's a
ring gear for the 1916 Buick. He always tries to stimulate
an answer of some sort, just to keep the channels open. To
receive all of his incoming mail, and it is a prodigious
amount, Charlie has rented a post-office box at Grend Central station. He shares it with four other fellows, just to
keep expenses down. Each morning he brings all the mail
to his desk and records in his notebooks whatever information is contained therein. Upon receipt of one of his communications, people inevitably say, "Good old Charlie. We
ought to have him out to dinner some night." If they say
this often enough, they usually do something about it.

It can easily be seen that a great deal of Charlie's time
is spent in keeping his notebooks up to date, making phone
calls, and writing brief communications. He is so busy that
he has to keep an engagement book labeled "Things to
do." If he gets a note from someone saying that little
Sammy has the mumps, he will enter a reminder in this
guide to action. A day or two later little Sammy will receive a "get well" card.

Charlie knows where he can get just about anything
free. He has a list of seven different penny scales around
Manhattan that will work without the insertion of a coin.
He is always quick to notice which people in his office
leave a package of life savers lying on their desks, and he

often arrives at the side of these people just at the moment they decide to take one. He not only observes which newspapers people read, but he knows where they are discarded, what time they are discarded, what their condition is, and who works what crossword puzzles. He likes the theater and the movies, but he has never seen the first act of a play or the first fifteen minutes of a movie since he's been in New York. If he wants to see a play, he simply arrives at the theater in time for the first intermission, mingles with the crowds in the lobby, and joins the standing room crowd when they file back into the auditorium. If there is an empty seat in the back of the house he will slip into it. He goes to the movies during the very last show, waits until the box office has closed and the ticket taker has disappeared, then saunters inside.

One of the problems which has caused Charlie the most trouble is transportation. Better than half the money he is forced to spend goes into subway or bus fares. He has never been able to figure out a way to get through a subway turnstile free, even though he has studied the situation carefully for some years. However, by keeping still another notebook, and applying his rule of volume, he has been able to whip the suburban situation and a few of the long distance metropolitan ride problems. He is just too busy and operates on too tight a schedule to walk anywhere. Wherever he works, he makes careful surveys of existing transportation opportunities and adds them to an ever-growing list which he constantly consults. He knows who owns automobiles, where they are parked, and on what routes they are used. He is able, if he wishes, to consult his notebook, make a telephone call, and get a ride to almost any place in the metropolitan area. In the summer, when he often spends week ends in the country, he can get a ride straight to the door of the house where he is to be a guest and another ride back to the city on Monday morning. According to his latest figures, he has more than 2,000 potential automobile rides. Like everything else he does, he starts making arrangements for rides well in advance. If he gets a dinner invitation for three weeks from Wednesday in Riverdale, he will immediately start sending out post cards or making phone calls to the people who drive out that way. On the day in question, he will slip out the door of the office where he is working, stand at the curb, and a car will glide up and take him in. There is rarely a slip-up in the schedule.

Charlie also collects information on commuters. When he accepts dinner invitations in nearby Jersey or Westchester, or on Long Island, he consults his transportation notebook, Commuter's Section. In every office in which he has ever worked, he has compiled a list of holders of commutation tickets. He also adds significant notes on these people. He knows that a great many of them stay in town for dinner or the theater every so often. When he receives an invitation to Short Hills, New Jersey, for instance, he flips the pages of his notebook to the Lackawanna subsection and starts calling people who are listed for Short Hills or beyond. When he finds one who expects to stay in town on the evening in question, he makes arrangements to meet his benefactor at some convenient point and pick up the ticket. At the close of the evening, there is always a second meeting at some agreed rendezvous point, and the ticket is returned. In the meantime, Charlie will have journeyed to Short Hills, had his dinner, spent an hour or two with his friends, and returned to town. He has traveled to virtually every point in Westchester, Long Island, and New Jersey without the expenditure of a cent other than subway or tube fares.

Charlie is often forced by the pressure of time to use taxicabs when he gets out of work. To keep from paying for them, he keeps a list of habitual cab users in every office in which he has worked. When in a hurry, he simply arrives at the curb just as one of these people is climbing into a taxi. He is usually invited to get in. If he can't find a cab rider in the office in which he is currently working, the chances are he knows someone in a company a block or two away where he used to work. He usually employs cabs to get across town in a hurry.

All of Charlie's efforts in saving money, which he accomplishes by making telephone calls, sending notes, and keeping lists, are directed towards his one goal in life—the Metropolitan Opera. He is a singer and he has never wavered in his belief that he is destined for glory on the opera stage. The bug bit him fifteen years ago when he was a sophomore at the State University of Iowa and a tenor in the glee club. He once sang a solo in Cedar Rapids, and the critics there said he ought to be in the Metropolitan. In 1946, after four years in the Navy, Charlie's ship made New York its final port of call. Charlie made it his, also. Since his discharge from service, he has pursued his singing career with single-mindedness and determination. The basic idea is to hold out for the big break. Charlie lives to get through one more meal, one more night's sleep. After the next payday, perhaps, the break will come. The only modification that has ever appeared in his program came not long ago when he confided to a friend that he would accept the lead in a Broadway musical if such an opportunity came along, and there are indications that he has recently softened his resistance towards movies and TV. He dreams about singing at night and talks about it in his waking hours. He gets his enjoyment from hearing other singers, he reads only about singers, and he dates only girls who are singers. Such plans as he has confided to me regarding marriage involve no one but divas.

A singing career requires a vast amount of training. Charlie would like to go to Italy to study, but he's never had enough money to make it. He takes his singing lessons in New York, therefore, and practices several hours a week. He must know languages to sing opera, so he takes lessons in French or Italian each week. He also takes dancing lessons and acting lessons, and because he intends to perform in a medium that is rich in the folklore of other countries, he feels it necessary to enroll in night school courses at one or another of New York's colleges or universities. There he studies history and literature. In ten years, Charlie has taken lessons from twenty-eight different singing teachers, including some of the world's foremost voice coaches. Whenever he hears that some new and famous teacher is arriving in this country from aboard, Charlie meets the boat. He is always looking for the teacher who can best bring out the quality in his voice. What that quality is, he doesn't know, but he says he will know when he finds it. While he waits, he goes right on studying.

Singing lessons with world famous teachers can be expensive. So are the language lessons, for Charlie is far beyond elementary language courses and he now studies with private tutors. The dancing and acting lessons, the tuition at night school, and the books all demand money. To practice every day, most serious singers rent studios. There is a whole section of New York along Broadway in the Seventies given over to these studios. A person can walk along the street at almost any time between the hours of eight in the morning and midnight and listen to arias and a lot of good solid scale exercises. In order to save money, Charlie usually rents his studio for an hour late at night when most other singers are home in bed, but even at reduced rates, it costs him quite a lot.

Charlie finances his future operatic career from the jobs he holds. In all the ten years he has been in New York, despite his constant changing from one job to another, he has never been out of work for more than one day at a time. Some of his jobs have paid extremely well. On one he made $150 a week. In addition to the regular jobs at which he generally works eight hours a day, five days a week, Charlie has additional income. He has been a member of a choral group that sings regularly on the radio. For his two hours of rehearsal and his one hour recording session each month, he receives an average of $25 a week. On each Saturday morning, for the last seven years, he has sung in a West Side synagogue. For this chore he receives $15 each week. On Sunday mornings he is a soloist in the choir of one of Manhattan's leading Presbyterian churches. He has to rehearse for two hours a week with the choir and must practice his solo on his own time, but the job pays him another $25. All of this practice and all of these lessons he weaves into his daily schedule, jumping from lesson to dinner to pets to practice, and never missing an appointment. As he moves around he carries his five or six notebooks with him, checking his progress against the "Things to do" pages.

In the ten years he has been in New York, Charlie has had countless auditions of one kind or another, but he never seems to get a start in his chosen profession. He has not so much as carried a spear onto the stage at the Met. This would discourage any normal person, but Charlie seems not in the least bit worried. He goes along each day at his frenzied pace. He could have had a hundred excellent jobs, if not more. Not long ago I pressed him to take an unusually high salaried position he had been offered with an oil company. Charlie demurred. He was still interested in only one thing.

"Do you still think you're going to make it, Charlie, after ten years?" I asked.

"Gosh," Charlie said. "Has it been that long?"

The Girl Who Wore No Clothes

In the summer of 1953, shortly after I had taken a job on the waterfront, I moved into an establishment I shall call the Hotel Crillon on the upper West Side. I was assigned to a small, clean room on the nineteenth floor that faced on an inner court. I could scarcely afford the room. Indeed, after paying for it and my food every week I rarely had anything left over. I was so broke most of the time that I had to sit in my one armchair and look at the bricks of the wing across the court. By the time I had been in residence for two weeks I knew most of the details of life in the part of the hotel that faced my window, with the exception of the room directly opposite mine. The only sign of residence in that room was on the window sill. There I could see three or four containers of the sort that hold cottage cheese or yogurt. As far as I could determine, these cartons were never disturbed, yet I knew they must have been because there was a different-colored one sometimes when I came home from work in the evening. Behind them, heavy drapes covered the window at all times, never admitting any breeze, and never allowing even the slightest crack of light to escape. I assumed that the occupant of the room was one of those very old ladies who inhabit New York hotels, hoarding small incomes, and sitting in the dark to relive a happier past.

I might never have found out anything about my neighbor if it had not been for a friend who came up to see me in the evenings. His name was George Brothers and he was a big, burly, muscle-flexer who fancied himself a lady-killer. He usually brought along three or four cans of beer and sat in my armchair, his feet propped up on the window sill, telling me about his latest conquests while I kept on doing whatever it was I had to do at the moment, paying no attention. One evening, toward the end of July, George was bragging and I was in the bathroom, perfecting the knot in my tie. All of a sudden he stopped talking in the middle of a sentence.

"Hey," he said to me. "Who's that?"

"Who's who?" I asked him from my place in front of the mirror.

"A dame just stuck her arm out of that curtain over there and grabbed something off the window sill," he said.

"Don't get excited," I told him. "This place is full of old women, and that's one of them."

"This was a young dame," George said, "and she looked like she didn't have any clothes on. You better keep your eyes open."

The rumored presence of a young, unclothed female was enough to arouse my curiosity, and I found my eyes drawn to the curtains across the court. Almost a week passed before I saw what George had seen. One Saturday morning I suddenly saw a long, well-shaped arm reach out and fumble along the window sill for one of the containers. When the hand did not readily grasp anything, the curtains parted further and a head of very beautiful auburn hair appeared. I didn't see the girl's face. I didn't need to.

The Hotel Crillon had a swimming pool that was available to guests, and I often used it. A few days after I first saw the auburn hair, I noticed a tall, perfectly formed woman in a tight, navy-blue bathing suit dive off the high board and swim to the shallow end of the pool. After she had slowly crawled up on the rim and perched herself there, she took off her bathing cap and shook out her hair. There was no mistaking who she was. I maneuvered around in the pool until I managed to get near her. I was trying to think of some way to strike up a conversation when she smiled down at me.

"Hello," she said. "I thought you'd be down here."

"You mean you know who I am?" I asked her.

"I know every muscle you have," she said. "Why don't you ever pull down your curtain?"

Her name was Martha Grant. We talked idly, saying nothing for about a half-hour or so. I didn't feel that I'd accomplished much, and I was quite pleasantly surprised, therefore, when my phone rang the next evening.

"I couldn't help noticing that you were going out," Martha said, "and I wondered if you'd mind very much doing me a favor."

"Not at all," I said.

"I don't feel like getting dressed up and going out, so I'd like to order a meal at the restaurant down at the corner. I wonder if you'd mind picking it up on your way in." I must have stammered a bit, because she seemed to read my mind. "There's no hurry about it," she said. "They're open until two in the morning, and I'm not especially hungry."

As a matter of fact, I hadn't intended to come home very early, but I couldn't tell her that. When a gentleman agrees to do a lady a favor, he does not impose a lot of conditions, especially if the lady is as good-looking as Martha Grant. I decided that the only decent thing to do was to pick up the food and then go about my business. When I got back to her room, I found a note on her door. "In pool," it said. "Be back in half an hour." I put the box with the food in it down in front of the door and went my way. She called me the next morning to thank me.

"I had no idea you'd be back so soon," she told me. "How much do I owe you?"

"Two dollars," I said. "Don't worry about it."

"Oh, but I will. Are you going for a swim this afternoon?"

"I could," I said.

I met her in the pool, but she didn't bring the money. There was something about the way she looked in that bathing suit that made it seem just a little incongruous to ask her for it. There was something tantalizing about her that drove monetary thoughts from one's mind. She had a way of getting you to do things voluntarily. That same afternoon, on the way back to the elevators, we passed the hotel's drugstore, which had a snack bar.

"Mmmmmmmmmm," Martha said, when we passed the door. "Hot dogs."

"Come on," I said. "I'll buy you one."

Martha ate four of them. She drank two glasses of milk. She ate a piece of pie alamode. And she drank two cups of coffee. Together with my Coke, the whole bill came to $2.15. I had to sign a chit to be added to my hotel bill.

I guess it was that chit that got me in trouble with the hotel. I was so broke at the moment that I hadn't been able to pay my hotel bill. It was two days overdue and, although my payday was only two days away, I was already a little uncomfortable about it. The very next evening when I returned from work, the credit manager called me on the phone. He wanted to know when I was going to pay my bill. I explained about my payday and promised to give him the money the next afternoon.

"All right," he said. "I'll expect to see you. In the meantime, please do not charge anything more to your bill."

I was embarrassed, but I was also angry, and the more I thought about it, the angrier I got, pacing the floor and muttering to myself about how honest I was. I was almost at the point of calling the credit manager back and giving him a piece of my mind when the phone rang. It was Martha, but there was something a little different about the way she sounded. Before, she had been all soft, alluring womanhood. Now there was something coldly matter-of-fact in her voice, a little on the schoolteacher side.

"Would you mind coming over here a moment?" she asked me, adding, "It's important."

I walked around to the other wing and knocked on the door of room 1904. It opened a crack and Martha looked out. I could see that her head was wrapped, turban-fashion, in a bath towel. After she'd slipped the bolt and opened the door wider to let me in, I discovered that she was clad *only* in towels. In addition to the one on her head, there was another one, arranged as sort of a makeshift sarong. It started just below her shoulders, and ended just above her knees. There was a slit that opened up the side, exposing glimpses of skin all the way to her hip. It was no place for an unbalanced man. I was so busy trying to get a good look at her that I didn't get a chance to observe the room fully. I do remember that it was dingy. It was dark, lighted only by a very dim bulb in the overhead fixture in the center of the ceiling. It was as hot as a steam bath. The bed had only a wrinkled sheet on it. There was a book lying open, face down, near the foot of the bed, and there was a bath towel thrown carelessly over the back of the chair at the desk. The room gave the impression of being littered.

Martha motioned me to the easy chair beside the drapes and then sat on the edge of the bed. She seemed utterly unconscious of the fact that she was seductively clad, and she wasted no time with amenities.

"Are you in trouble with the hotel?" she asked me.

"Why?" I asked her.

"Because the credit manager was snooping around your room this morning," she said.

"He was?" I sat up in the chair. "What was he doing?"

"He was counting your possessions."

I stood up. "He can't get away with that," I blurted out. "That's none of his damned business."

Martha smiled, a little cynically.

"You don't know hotels very well," she said. "Sit down and calm down. It isn't going to do any good to get mad. Here! Let me give you a little lesson about hotels." She got up and walked over to her closet. In a moment she pulled out a bundle of clothes. She brought them over to me and held out a dress on a hanger, indicating that I should look at it. It was full of holes and absolutely unwearable. I scratched my head.

"Credit managers *count* clothes—they don't inspect them," she said. "I got these at the Salvation Army, and if you're going to live in a hotel on a shoestring, I'd advise you to do the same thing. Fill up the closets and look prosperous." She walked to the closet and put the clothes back in, then came over to the writing desk and picked up a piece of paper that was lying there. I found myself looking at a cashier's check for $500. "I always leave this lying around in plain sight," she said. "It isn't any good. I had a friend of mine make it up for me. But it makes a good impression, and a credit manager's eyes will always pop out when he sees it." She threw the check carelessly back on the desk. "I always leave a few well-figured bankbooks and check stubs lying around, too. I've written down a few simple rules for you to follow. If you look at them and live up to them, you'll never get in trouble with a hotel and you can live in one practically indefinitely on nothing." She went over to her pillow and took an envelope out from under it, handing it to me. I was just unfolding it when there was a knock on the door. Martha stood in the center of the floor, looking at me speculatively.

"Do you have *any* money at all?"

"A little," I said, sheepishly.

"About $1.65?"

"I guess so," I said, reluctantly reaching in my pocket.

Martha opened the door a crack. I could see a boy standing there with a box. I knew it was a dinner because it was the same kind of box I had brought up from the restaurant. After she'd paid for it with my money, she turned to face me again. Her manner seemed to be softer and more sympathetic.

"I'm sorry I had to do that to you," she said. "Now that I now you're busted, I won't do it again. I wouldn't have done it tonight except that I had already called the restaurant before I knew, and I didn't want to send the dinner back." She moved toward the door and put her hand on the knob. It was a plain invitation to leave. "Be sure and study those rules," she said. "If you have any questions, call me."

"I do have one question," I said, as I stood in the hall. "Don't you ever wear any clothes in here?"

She looked down at herself and fingered the towels, then looked up at me, archly. "Only this," she said, "and then only when I have company."

The first rule on the list she had given me was never to sign a chit for anything. I was never to discuss my financial affairs on the telephone and never to promise anybody on the hotel staff anything. I wasn't to fraternize with any of the hotel's employees, and never sit in the lobby. I was still looking over some of the rules when George Brothers arrived.

"Where do you think I've just been?" I asked triumphantly. Then, without waiting for an answer, I jerked my head toward the window across the court.

"No kidding?" He went to the window and leaned there, peering across at the heavy drapes. When he turned around, he looked a little lascivious. "Any clothes?"

I smiled knowingly. He grinned back at me. Then, suddenly, a cloud came over his face.

"What were you doing over there then?"

"She wrapped herself up in a towel to receive me."

"Oh," George said, brightening a little. "Is she good-looking?"

"Damned good-looking."

"How about an introduction?" he asked me.

"Wait'll I get to know her better," I told him.

The discovery that I was not as wealthy as she had thought put me in a new category with Martha. I became a fellow conspirator instead of a suitor, and the conspiring began almost immediately. George had no sooner finished his beer and departed when my phone rang. It was Martha.

"Who was that big gorilla staring at my window?" she wanted to know.

"His name is George Brothers. He thinks you're cute."

"How does he know?"

"He saw your arm and shoulder reaching through the curtain one day. He thinks there is something attractive about the idea of your not ever wearing any clothes. He wants to meet you."

"Hmmmmmmmm," she said. "You better have him call me up."

I don't know how many days in a row George took Martha out, or how many meals he bought her. He didn't complain to me about that. What he did complain about was the fact that he was never able to get into that room. He was always forced to stand out in the hall while she talked demurely to him through the crack in the door. She always had that towel around her head, and she sometimes managed to stick one bare arm out into the hall so that George could hold her hand. On one such occasion, I gathered, the other towel had dropped off while she was thus engaged. George got only a glimpse of bare flesh, but it was enough to fan the flame of his interest into a conflagration. He was enthusiastic. He was so enthusiastic that when he ran into Martha on the way to the swimming pool a few hours later, he lent her $15. She had left her billfold up in her room and hated to run all the way back upstairs for it. As far as I knew he never got it back.

Martha never let him off the hook, either. He would be in my room complaining about how he wasn't getting anywhere with her when the curtain across the court would part and there would be that bare arm, reaching for a box of yogurt. Naturally, the curtain would always slip a little, revealing a considerable expanse of bare shoulder and a glimpse of something else. George would be on my phone in a minute, and he'd always end up with an order for a carton of chop suey or a ham sandwich.

"Well," he'd say, when he left, "I gotta go. Maybe she'll let me in when I come back. If you see a hand wave, you'll know I made it."

Martha discussed George with me once or twice. About a week after he'd first telephoned, she called me over to her room. I found her clad in her towels, as usual.

"What about this George?" she asked me.

"I can tell you one thing," I told her. "You better not let him in this room."

"Has he got enough money to make it worth my while to get caught in a wrestling match with him?"

"He's an organizer for the International Longshoremens Association."

"A real good friend of yours?"

"Just an acquaintance," I said.

She sat there on the bed, thinking.

"He ought to be good for about $100," she finally said. "You mustn't be offended if I take him for that much."

"Supposing I warn him?" I asked her. "After all, I'm a man and I have a certain loyalty to my sex."

"He's a jerk," she said. "If you want to protect him, go ahead."

"What makes you think he's a jerk?"

"He's playing a game that he thinks he invented. He's interested in only one thing, and he thinks he's going to get it without giving up anything important. He pretends he's in love. He calls me up all the time and makes believe he's being thoughtful and considerate when all the time he's painting a great big picture in his mind of what I look like while I'm sitting here talking to him. Well, I'm interested in one thing, too. It's money, and if I can take him without his taking me, why shouldn't I?"

Martha didn't take George for the hundred dollars all at once. She took him for it two or three dollars at a time. And all the while she was doing it, he was feeding her at least a meal a day, two a day on week ends. I kept waiting for him to complain about it, but he never did. He just fretted because he wasn't getting anywhere. When I thought he'd had enough, I went over to see Martha again.

"I have to make a living some way," she told me.

"Wouldn't it be easier if you went out and got a job?" I asked her.

All at once she stopped being a capable, poised woman and became a frightened little girl.

"I've worked," she told me, in a quiet voice. "I'm not afraid to work. I just can't ever stand it very long. I get sick. I have a very delicate constitution."

"I don't wonder that you have a very delicate constitution," I said, sweeping my arm around the room. "You sit here all day long without a breath of fresh air, with no sunlight, and without even the proper food to eat. The way you live would kill most people."

"I have to be careful," she said. "I can't go out in the sun."

"Why not?"

"I'm allergic to it."

"Allergic to the sun?" I stared at her.

"That's what my doctors say."

"Why don't you go out on a cloudy day, then?"

"I'd freeze. I'm anemic. I shudder when I even feel a little breeze."

"My God," I said. "What else are you allergic to? Clothes?"

"No," she said. "I have another reason for not wearing any clothes." She seemed to cheer up a bit. "Does it bother you?"

"I keep waiting for that towel to slip," I told her. "Aren't you afraid I might try to seduce you? It's a temptation. That slit in the lower part of it is disturbing."

"You couldn't seduce me."

"Why not?"

"People tell me it's painful, and I can't stand pain of any kind. My doctor tells me that I can't have babies because of that. The pain would drive me insane."

"You'd better change doctors," I told her. "The one you've got is ruining your life."

"Oh," she said, "it's not just one doctor that I depend on. I have several doctors and they all agree. My gynecologist is the one that told me about the babies. Besides, even if it weren't for the doctors, I know that what I say is true. I read a lot." She picked a book off the bed and showed it to me. It was open at about halfway through, to "Diseases of the Blood." Martha took the book back and waved at a row of books on her dresser. There were fifteen or twenty volumes there, all medical books of one kind or another.

"Do you read all those?" I asked her.

"Of course. All I ever read is medical books."

"Do you understand them?"

"I have to."

"Why?"

"I have so many things the matter with me that I have to know what to do in an emergency," she said.

About a week after this conversation, I decided to move out of the Crillon. I hadn't followed any of the suggestions that Martha had written down for me and, whether that was the reason or not, I had had three or four arguments with the credit manager. Things were just too unpleasant. After I had packed my own suitcase, I went around to the other wing to say good-by.

"Evicted?" Martha asked me, curiously.

"No," I said, "I'm just tired of the way they run this place."

"Well, let me know where you are," she said, a little wistfully. "I might need some help soon."

There was something about the way she said it that made me look at her more closely.

"Are you in trouble?" I asked her. For answer, she went over to her desk and brought a piece of paper to me. It was an eviction notice. I saw that she owed the hotel almost $200.

"Gee," I said. "I don't have anywhere near that amount of money or I . . ."

"I didn't really think you did," she sighed, and put the paper back.

"But what are you going to do?" I asked her. "You can't just go out and walk the streets."

"I won't walk the streets," she said. "I know what to do about this. If you'll just help me."

"But I don't have $200."

"I don't need money," she said. "All I need is help."

"All right," I said. "What do I do?"

She went over to her closet and came back with three dresses, a winter coat, and a pair of shoes.

"I have to get these things out of the hotel," she said. "Could you take them with you when you go? Drop the dresses at a cleaner's and keep the winter coat until I call you for it. You see," she explained, "I don't dare leave the place. They'd lock me out in a minute. And they won't let me take anything out when they finally do evict me. Of course, that won't be for quite a while yet." She walked back over to the closet and stood looking in, then she grabbed a whole armful of clothes and brought them over to me. "I might just as well get rid of these, too. Would you take them back over to your room with you? Just dump them on the bed or on the floor and call the Salvation Army and tell them you've left a bundle of clothes for them. They'll pick them up."

"What else?" I asked her.

"I won't make you do all my errands," she said. "Besides, there's George. He can take my laundry out, and I'll let him keep my books for me. You might have him call me on the phone."

"Why don't *you* call him?"

"Oh, he likes to call me. Let him have some fun."

I did not sever my connections with Martha. In the first place, I had her coat. In the second place, I had to take the cleaner's receipts back to her. And, lastly, she had more things she wanted me to do for her. She made me promise to call her. I found, very soon, that this meant calling her every day, to check in, after a fashion. George also brought me word or news each day. I went back to the Crillon for the first time about four days after I moved out. Afterward I went two or three times a week. I soon got into the habit of taking her a hot meal whenever I went, and I found that others were doing the same thing. It developed that she had acquired a few allies in her war with the Crillon management. One of the bellhops even brought her a box of groceries, which she kept in the bathtub and from which she munched occasionally. Everybody who came to see her not only brought her something, they also carried something away. Her shoes, an item of clothing, a book, or a trinket; it made no difference. Her possessions all left the premises, one by one. By the time of my third visit, the room was as bare as she was.

The eviction notice had instructed her to vacate the premises by September 27, as I recall. On the afternoon of that day the credit manager appeared at room 1904 at precisely three o'clock, which was check-out time. When Martha opened to his knock, he informed her that she would have to leave. She informed him that she had no intention of leaving, and slammed the door in his face. The next logical move, as far as the credit manager was concerned, was to lay siege. He sat in the lobby for several days, waiting in vain for her to go out so that he could plug the keyhole while she was gone. A steady stream of the necessities of life floated right by his chair and on up to room 1904.

As the siege lengthened, and its failure became apparent, the hotel management must have had some interesting conferences about what to do next. One month after she was supposed to have departed, Martha was still in the room, and the bill had soared to well over $300. At this point, the credit manager gave up waiting. He advanced on room 1904 one morning, accompanied by two burly and loyal house officers, intent upon carrying her bodily from the premises and depositing her in the street. He banged on the door and, when it opened a slit, he informed Martha that he was about to force his way in if she didn't grant him admittance. She replied that such a move would not be necessary. She retreated three steps, dropped her towels, and stood in the center of the room in a pose reminiscent of "September Morn." The two house officers thrust open the door, took one look, and backed out. The credit manager peeked his head in and abruptly withdrew. He then stood in the hall and demanded that Martha clothe herself. She informed him, in a very plaintive voice, that she couldn't. There wasn't a stitch in the place that she could put on. There was some disbelief expressed through the door, but every time Martha offered to let the men come in and see for themselves, they demurred. This was finally settled by letting a maid enter to inspect the premises. The maid verified Martha's contention. At that point the credit manager and the two house officers retired to the hotel offices for more conferences. Martha lay down on her bed to read her one remaining medical book.

For the next week there was a good deal of telephoning back and forth between room 1904 and the hotel offices. Martha started out by telling the hotel that she would leave, gladly, if they would get her some suitable clothes to wear. The hotel sent up a maid's uniform, and Martha sent it back with a note on which the word "suitable" was underlined. In between cajoling and threatening, the credit manager sent up five or six dresses. They were all sent back as being too small, too big, not warm enough, or not clean.

When everything else failed, the police were called in. The credit manager wanted the police to cart Martha out of the building and off to jail. He was vituperative, vehement, flushed, demanding, and not a little incoherent. The detective who was in charge of the case, like all policemen, had been instructed to do his duty, but he was also a reasonable man who realized that many disputes can be settled amicably without filling jails. In this particular case he was confronted by a wild, abusive man who waved his arms in the air and spouted a string of accusations that included fraud, vagrancy, prostitution, and grand larceny. He went up to room 1904, where he met Martha, who was clad in her towels. She sat and talked sweetly, calmly, and with reason, explaining to the detective that she would leave the hotel of her own free will, and had been willing to do so all along, but that she had been unable to do so because of the hotel itself. She had sent all her clothes out to be cleaned, preparatory to moving, and they had been picked up by a friend. Then the hotel had cut off her telephone, and she hadn't been able to reach her friend or anybody. Now she didn't know where her friend or her clothes were.

There must have been something about the way that Martha told this rather implausible story. Perhaps she had rehearsed it several times. She couldn't prove a word of it, it was full of all kinds of holes, and on top of everything she didn't have a legal leg to stand on, but that didn't make the slightest difference. She was reasonable, and the detective said he believed her. He didn't think she had any right to make any demands on the hotel, but in the back of his mind there lurked a conviction that she was somehow right and the credit manager wrong. He promised her that he would recommend that the hotel accept her solution. He also went out and bought her a meal. I arrived for one of my visits and heard the whole story that same night.

"You know," I told her, after listening patiently, "even if you get out of here without getting thrown in jail, you're still in trouble. What are you going to do without any money?"

"Oh," she said, "whatever gave you that idea? I have a little money. You forget that George has been more than generous, and one of the bellhops lent me $25. Even that nice detective shows some signs of chipping in a little. I think he feels sorry for me. Altogether, I think I'll have about $150 for the next step. That's plenty."

"The next step?" I asked her. "Just what is the next step?"

"Oh, that reminds me," she said, "I may need a little more of your help. Do you mind?"

"Okay," I said. "What do you want me to do?"

She sat down at her desk and got out a piece of paper. "Let me see," she said. "I'll need my green suit, and my black cocktail dress, and my nightie, and . . ." She began writing. "Do you have a suitcase?" she asked when she finally looked up at me.

"Yes," I said.

She came over to me with the slip of paper on which she'd been writing.

"Now these are the things I'm going to need," she said. "I've made it as easy for you as I can. The suit and two dresses that I've put down here are at a cleaner's a block from each other. The lingerie is all in the same bundle. It's at Lee Fong's on 94th Street. The only thing that you'll have any trouble with are the shoes. The black ones are at the cobbler's on 91st Street. The green ones are way over on the East Side."

"My God," I said.

"After you get all these things collected," she said, ignoring my remark, "pack them in the suitcase. I'll call you tomorrow if I get this mess straightened out, and tell you where to bring them."

She walked to the door with me. When I got there, she reached up and pulled my face down and kissed me lightly on the mouth. "You're a dear," she said, opening the door. "I'd give you the money to pay the cleaners, the laundry, and the cobblers, but I have my money in storage, too. Will that be all right?"

Martha called me the next afternoon and asked me to bring the suitcase to the Hotel Argyll on Madison Avenue. When I got there, I found her in the cocktail bar. She had on a devastating green jersey dress.

"You know," I said to her when I sat down, "this is the first time I ever saw you with clothes on."

"How do you like it?" She stood back for me to see.

"This is what the Crillon bought me, thanks to that detective."

I bought her a drink, a lemonade. She explained that she couldn't drink liquor because it gave her a headache, and she couldn't stand headaches.

"Don't you think the Argyll a little expensive for anyone with as little money as you have?" I asked her.

"I'll only be here a couple of days," she said. "I can afford that."

"Then where are you going?"

"Probably to a hospital," she said, and sighed.

"You can't afford that, either," I told her. "What's the trouble with you now?"

She seemed apprehensive, almost frightened.

"I have to have a wisdom tooth pulled," she said.

"You won't have to go to the hospital for *that*."

"You don't know me, and how pain affects me."

"Nonsense," I said. "It'll only be sore for a day or two."

"It isn't nonsense," she said. "And besides, I might bleed to death. My blood doesn't clot very well."

"Maybe the dentist won't pull it, then."

"You don't know much about dentists. I'll tell this dentist about my blood, and he'll just say that I'm trying to get out of having the tooth pulled. He'll laugh at me, just like you do, and then I'll bleed and bleed and bleed. Maybe I'll die."

"Nonsense," I said.

She put her hand on my arm, sorrowfully.

"Would you do me one more favor?" she said, softly. "It's the last one I'll ever ask. I promise."

"All right," I said.

"I have a prescription at a pharmacy on the lower West Side. Will you get it filled and bring it to the hospital when I call you?"

Martha called me from Mount Sinai two days later. I took the prescription and went to see her. There was no acting in the discomfort she professed. She was in pain, and really miserable.

"I warned the dentist," she said, "but he knew more than I did and went ahead and pulled the tooth. Now they can't stop the bleeding. Did you bring the prescription?"

"Yes," I said, then looked at her sternly. "Martha, this isn't for the relief of pain."

"Who said it was?"

"This is an anticoagulant. The druggist told me." I reached for her hand, to pat it. "Martha, you're not dealing with a chain hotel, now. This is a dentist you've got paying through the nose for this mistake he thinks he's made. He's probably married and got a family to support. Why don't you give it up and live like anybody else?"

Martha brushed my hand away and looked up at me. Her eyes weren't soft any more.

"This dentist happens to be rich," she said. "It took me a long time to find him. What's more, he's a wolf. He made a pass at me while I was in his chair, and he intends to make more. He drools every time he comes in here to see me. Stop worrying about my ethics." She turned over with her face to the wall. I got up and left.

I probably wouldn't have seen Martha again except that I had to get my suitcase back. She called me one day and told me where to come to get it. I found her living in a small residential hotel on Gramercy Park. Her room there was about the same as the one at the Crillon. When I arrived, she was fully dressed. She had on a cocktail dress and a chic little hat. She told me she was going out for dinner. When she went to the closet to get out the suitcase, I got a glimpse of what she had been doing while she waited for me to come. Two of the hotel towels were stuffed behind the chair. There were a needle and thread on top of them. She had been sewing them together.

"Guess who's taking me to dinner," Martha said to me, ignoring the fact that I was holding up the towels to look at them.

"The dentist," I said.

"Oh, no," she said. "He paid for my room for a month. I really couldn't ask him for anything more after all he's done for me."

"George?"

"No," she said. "It's that nice detective I met at the Crillon. He's been real good to me."

Saint Dutch: The Body Snatcher

During 1952 and 1953 while I was working on various jobs along the waterfront, I began to hear about a man named Father Dutch. Bums throughout the area could tell many stories about him. I talked to several small boys near the Cunard piers and they knew him, too. But his fame was not limited to New York. In 1956 on a train from San Francisco, I met a Jesuit priest who had spent several years in China. He, too, knew Father Dutch, and told me more stories about him. Father Dutch was on his way to becoming a legend.

Father Dutch was a sturdy man with crew-cut yellow hair and a round, grinning face. He was just below six feet in height and built on a broad, sturdy base. He was as hard, physically, as he seemed to be emotionally. He loved to crunch a man's hand in his until the man winced. There weren't any whiners within ten blocks of Dutch at any given time because he wouldn't allow it. He'd either frighten them away quickly, or kid them out of feeling sorry for themselves.

"Go ahead and jump in the river," he told one man, "and see if I care. See if anybody cares. You might just as well face it. If they don't care for you now, when you're alive, they sure aren't going to give two hoots for you when you're dead."

Father Dutch was a Jesuit priest once. He'd spent four years as a prisoner of the Japanese and three years as a prisoner of the Chinese Communists in China. He'd been pretty banged up and hadn't been fed much during his captivity. When he got back to the United States in 1949, he'd had to undergo three major operations to correct the damage that had been done to him. In August of 1950, while recuperating from the last of these, he stepped through the hedge of a rest home in Boston, and disappeared. Church authorities did not learn what had become of him until five years later.

A lot of people, especially on New York's West Side, thought that Father Dutch was mentally unbalanced. The police referred to him, unofficially, as the Body Snatcher, a name that was sometimes applied also by small boys. No one ever did anything about him because he was always good for a laugh. On top of that, no one was quite sure about Dutch's sanity. There was always the possibility that he was right; he was certainly sincere and determined enough to evoke a good deal of admiration and a genuine feeling of friendship.

Dutch talked often about God. He talked about God with a familiarity and certainty that lent authority to his utterances, and this probably accounted for some of the skepticism with which his mental condition was viewed. According to Dutch, God was responsible for his being in New York. He'd just started to walk in Boston, and he kept on walking until God told him to stop. The reason he knew he was supposed to stay in New York was simple. He'd been walking through towns and cities all the way through Connecticut. He'd go in one end and come out the other. When he got to New York, he just couldn't find his way out. After wandering around the streets for three days, he just decided that he was supposed to stay. So he did.

Father Dutch had never been in New York City before. He didn't know a soul, and he didn't have a penny in his pockets. Five minutes after he'd made up his mind to stay, he found himself standing in front of a restaurant that needed a bus boy. He worked long enough to collect one meal and a piece of information. One of his fellow workers suggested that he visit a certain mission on West 42nd Street if he wanted a place to sleep for the night. For the next two years this mission, and others like it, became the hub around which Dutch's life revolved. The number of missions operating in New York varies from week to week, but at any one time fifty would be a good estimate. They are maintained by government agencies, private foundations, individuals, and religious organizations. They furnish a varied list of services. Most important of these are food and shelter. Some of them, in addition, have recreation facilities, some have employment agencies, and some are equipped with social workers who try to solve problems. All of them are staffed by unselfish people who do what they can for the men who come to them for help.

At first, after he found out about the missions, Father Dutch was content to eat and sleep in them, and to use such facilities as they offered. He later remarked that it was simply a case of not knowing where else to go. For three or four months he left them each morning to return at night. During the daylight hours he wandered through the city, getting to know it. It was something of an orientation period. Shortly after New Year's, 1951, the city was struck by a severe cold spell. On the first night of it, the mission where he was staying filled up with homeless men before nine o'clock, and the workers in charge began turning them away.

"I suddenly realized," Dutch recalled later, "that I was taking up room that rightfully belonged to someone else. I was not an object of charity, and these other men were."

He got up from his chair in the recreation room of the mission, put on his overcoat, and stepped out into the night. For the next year and a half, Father Dutch went through what he called his "empty building" period.

"I didn't know where I was going or what I was going to do," he said. "All I knew was that it was awful cold and that I'd better keep moving. I just walked up one street and down the other. New York can be awfully lonely and dark on a bitter night, and this night was no exception. There wasn't a person anywhere in sight. On either side of me there were buildings that rose up for tens of stories. The longer I walked, the more I thought about it. Here were all these buildings, heated, and comfortable and *empty*. All the people who worked in them had gone home hours before and left them alone. It seemed like an awful waste to me because I'd just seen a lot of people who didn't have any place to go to get out of the cold."

Dutch was a man of action. He began trying doors. When he found one that was open, he would walk into the lobby and stand around getting warm. The next night he did the same thing. As time passed, he became something of an authority on empty buildings. He knew where he could gain entrance and where he couldn't. He knew where he would be kicked out, if found, and he knew how much liberty he could take in buildings where he was allowed to remain. In some of them he had a little niche where he habitually sank down out of sight with his back up against the marble wall, and slept. In others, he stretched out on a sofa in some reception room where a watchman allowed him to stay.

Although he no longer occupied beds in the missions, Father Dutch continued to eat his meals in them and hung around them in the early evenings. He soon got into the habit of appearing at one or another of them around four o'clock in the afternoon and going to work. He did all the dirty jobs, mopping the floor, scrubbing the pots and pans, and peeling the potatoes. After he'd finished his work, and after everyone else had been fed, he would take a meal himself, then go out into the recreation room of the mission and play cribbage or checkers. He would ordinarily stay at one mission for a week, then move on to another one.

Father Dutch led an aimless sort of existence for quite a long time. He was in the habit of shrugging his shoulders, when discussing these early days with me, and saying that he had been waiting for God to show him what to do.

Father Dutch set a great deal of store by cleanliness. When he had walked out of the convalescent home in Boston, he was wearing his black clerical trousers, black shoes, and an old maroon-colored corduroy lounging jacket. He had on no shirt or hat, but on his way through Connecticut he had been given a bright, checked sports shirt, and an old, worn, slouch hat. He did not vary this wardrobe, except for adding an old overcoat, until something wore out. At least twice a week, however, during his first year in New York, he would retire to the basement of the missions and wash out his clothing. Before long he began to wear holes in almost everything he had. In most of the missions there were supplies of clothing on which he could have drawn, but he steadfastly refused to take anything that belonged to the needy. Instead, he would mend what he had.

On certain nights during each week, ladies of the churches that supported most of the missions might give an hour or two to help the men who congregated there. They would write letters, or sew, or read aloud. Dutch decided to take sewing lessons. He not only became adept with a needle and thread, but he also learned how to use a sewing machine, how to darn socks, and knit. He later visited a tailor and learned something about weaving and fitting cloth. On many evenings he sat alongside the ladies and did his share of the sewing. During the winter of 1951-1952, he started carrying a sewing kit around in his pocket. Five or six times a day, in his wandering, he would run across some vagrant with a rent in his pants, or with buttons or zippers missing in important places. He would escort his find to the nearest park bench and make such emergency repairs as were necessary. In addition to this, he became one of the few bums who ever carried his knitting around with him. When he became tired of wandering during the day, he would sit down, take needles and yarn out of an old paper bag, and work while he rested. He made a red stocking cap for himself and wore it most of the time. He knitted all his own socks, a sweater, and several pairs of mittens. Toward the end of his third year, he was practically mass-producing mittens for bums he met. At one time he seriously considered learning how to repair shoes, but he gave this up because he lacked the facilities and materials to practice the trade.

As time passed, Father Dutch became increasingly aware of the bums around him.

"I had no idea how many men were in need of help in this city," he once said. "They were everywhere I turned. I was constantly thrown together with them in the missions, but before long I realized there were hundreds, perhaps thousands, who never came near a mission at all. Some of them have too much pride to take charity. Some are just too resourceful. They have money in their pockets and they can do better for themselves outside a mission, but they need help, anyway. And then there are some that are just plain derelicts. There are some bums in New York that even other bums won't have anything to do with. They're the ones that you see lying in the gutter on a steaming hot afternoon, or freezing in a doorway on a bitter cold night, dead drunk. They always end up in Bellevue or the East River. They never come to the missions because they aren't welcome, either among the social workers, or the other bums."

Although Father Dutch became interested in all bums,

he spent most of his time studying the drunks. He sought out the places where he knew he could find them and discovered that their preference was vacant buildings. They wanted places where they could take a bottle of wine or cheap whiskey and lean up against a wall and be comfortable. Sometimes they drank alone, but usually there would be two or three of them together. Dutch spent a good many nights huddled in a dark corner, out of sight, listening to the garbled reminiscences and drunken plans that were spun out until the bottle was gone.

"The directors of the missions and the social workers are experts in the fields of alcoholism," Dutch declared. "They are all earnest and sincere people. I talked with most of them and tried to learn from them, but I soon came to be conscious of something that I don't think they were conscious of themselves. They professed to want to help these men, but what they really wanted to do was reform them. Help and reform were synonymous. Whenever they came across a man who admitted that he was helpless, and who hoped to rejoin respectable society, the forces of charity would swoop down on him in legions. It was like a field army rushing in to break up a street corner altercation. There aren't very many alcoholics who really want to reform. Most of them are cynical, depraved, dishonest, and obscene men. They just want to be left alone to die, and they make fun of the people who try to help them because they want none of your reform. Any number of social workers have pointed out men to me as being beyond help, or not wanting help. What they really meant was that the man was beyond reform, or incorrigible. When I see a man lying on the sidewalk in the hot sun, I know he can be helped. He can be moved into the shade. When I see a man lying in the doorway on a bitter cold night, I know he can be helped. He can be moved to a warm place before he freezes to death. That much has nothing to do with reform."

Two years and two months after he first came to New York, Father Dutch decided that he knew why God had sent him to the city. It was to cake care of drunks. He has since recalled that his original conception of the job involved getting a mission building with beds and a kitchen. At first he thought of himself as the shepherd of all the drunks on Manhattan Island. He soon modified his ideas.

"People get drunk all over New York," he said one day, "but if you do much reading on the subject, you will soon get the idea that the only drunken bums in the world are on the Bowery. I looked New York over pretty carefully, and I finally decided that the lower East Side was filled with people who were either drunk or taking care of drunks. I didn't think I could add anything to what was being done there, so I decided to go some place else. The West Side is fertile ground, especially along the water front, but it extends a long way. I went over there and walked all the way from the Battery to the 125th Street ferry. I walked it in the forenoons and in the afternoons. I walked it in the early evening and in the early morning. I decided that I couldn't begin to take care of all of it, so I narrowed it down. I made up my mind that whatever area I took, I ought to be able to cover it three times a day, so I started out and walked as far as I could in five hours, between Ninth and Twelfth Avenues. I walked up one crosstown street and down another. When I was all done, I decided I would establish my mission between 32nd Street and 61st Street, between Ninth Avenue and the docks."

Father Dutch didn't have any money, but he knew he would need some in his work so he turned his attention to this problem.

"There was one bum who used to come into the Salvation Army mission I used to work at," Dutch recalled. "He was the most successful bum I ever knew. He'd go to the busiest corner he could find at the busiest time of day and thread his way through this pack of people. He'd keep up a rapid fire of talk. He'd argue with some, implore, get angry, and just plain browbeat. He'd go through a crowd and come out the other side with two or three dollars. That was for me."

Dutch traveled all over Manhattan, starting out each day at eleven o'clock and working until two in the afternoon. One day he would hit one of the midtown corners, the next he'd travel downtown. He'd collect between eight and ten dollars every noon. He never used any of the money on himself, except for subway or bus fare to and from his collecting point. He was not afraid to walk, and would have, except that he felt guilty using valuable time. All his time was valuable. Fulfilling his own needs took a good deal of it because he was still working in the missions for his meals and still wandering about town to find a place to sleep each night, but the longer he worked in his mission area, the less time he had, even for himself.

Most of the money that Father Dutch collected went for food. He had a theory that a man with a full belly would be much more likely to calm down and sleep. Since most derelicts have bad stomachs and severe cases of the shakes, Dutch tried to pour as much milk down them as possible. He found out that a drunk who had passed out was likely to wake up after three or four fitful hours of sleep. If, when he woke up, he would eat a big meal, he might go back to sleep and rest for fifteen or twenty hours. Some of the men who took Dutch's patented cure hung around with him for a week or more, eating the oversized meals that Dutch provided and sleeping for eight or ten hours a day. It was not a case of getting a man off a binge, although this often happened. What Dutch was interested in was making his patient feel better. Some of Dutch's carefully accumulated money went to purchase good whiskey. He understood that the only thing that could get some men on their feet and going again after a long bout was a shot of liquor.

Aside from food and money, Dutch's main concern was shelter. For several months after he had settled on his mission area, he explored it thoroughly. He'd learned a good deal about empty (in use but unoccupied at certain hours) and vacant (not in use) buildings in his first two years in New York, and he could usually tell at a glance which ones were warm and comfortable, and which ones were protected by watchmen and alarm devices. The part of town in which Father Dutch had chosen to operate is run down and full of marginal buildings. At almost any given moment there are from fifty to one hundred vacant in the area, ranging all the way from boarded-up and condemned tenement buildings to modern loft buildings in temporary disuse. Dutch investigated every one. He tried the doors, examined the basement windows, tested the boarding on the condemned structures, and inspected the fire escapes. Whenever he found that he could get inside—and there was scarcely a building that he couldn't get into—he explored it carefully from basement to skylight. If there was an elevator that was working, he tried it out. If there was a pile of refuse, he found out what was in it. Some of the more objectionable messes he cleaned up himself, if they weren't too large. He wanted to know everything about every one of these buildings, and made periodic checks to make sure that nothing had changed.

Over a long period, Father Dutch tried to call on the owners or agents of all of the buildings he had explored. He explained what he wanted and sought permission to use them as temporary shelter for the men he was trying to help. Refusal of permission did not deter him, however. He used most of the buildings anyway. Out of all his calls, he received help from only one man, the manager of a large bakery, but this help was impressive. The manager himself was a reformed alcoholic, and he was immediately interested in what Dutch was trying to do. The bakery was a seven-story building, swarming with activity, but the manager was kind enough to make a small room available. It had its own entrance on Tenth Avenue and had, at one time, been used to store maintenance equipment. Steampipes ran through it, making it quite warm and cozy. At first, Dutch was given permission merely to haul a bum in off the street and keep him in the room under surveillance, but as the manager became more and more aware of Father Dutch's activities, he expanded the uses to which the room might be put. Out of his own pocket, he installed a cot, a stove, a sink, and an electric refrigerator.

The acquisition of the bakery room did a great deal to change Father Dutch's life. He gave up working in the missions and slept on the cot. This gave him a great deal more time. From the spring of 1954 on, he cooked meals for his bums and for himself on the stove. He was not a good cook, but he did learn how to make a palatable stew, and there was almost always a big pot of it simmering on the stove. Now his money went a great deal further because he no longer had to take his patients to restaurants and feed them. He could also get the drunks out of the vacant buildings to which he had temporarily hauled them, and into more comfortable quarters.

Father Dutch's theory of handling drunks was a relatively simple one. His sole purpose was to administer comfort. He did not think of the drunks as criminals or cases to be studied. For that reason he liked to keep them out of the hands of authority. He made it a rule always to get a bum before the patrol wagon did, and, in order to do so, he soon established a rather elaborate alarm system, manned principally by bums who knew him and appreciated what he was doing, or by children who generally got a quarter for every drunk rescued.

Father Dutch began his work at dawn each morning. At that time he generally made a complete round of his entire district, looking for drunks. He looked for them on the street, and he delved into the little nooks and crannies where they might have stumbled and fallen. He visited every bar and every back alley. By the end of his round, when it was time for him to go in search of money, he had cleaned up most of the results of the previous night's debauchery and he also knew, pretty well, what drinking was taking place in the area. He never went near a drunk who was still on his feet, but he was a keen appraiser of those that had only a limited amount of time left. As a man neared capacity, Dutch often posted a watch over him. A short time after a man went down, Dutch was at hand. When he had returned from his panhandling, Dutch would make another round of the area, reassessing the situation, and then lie down and take a nap until early evening. Once it got dark he was usually on the go until the last bar closed. Then, if there was still an hour or two until daylight, he might sleep again. Sometimes, because a sobering drunk was in his bed, Dutch slept on the floor.

Father Dutch had a fairly regular routine in handling his drunks. When notified that a man had passed out in De Witt Clinton Park, or on Tenth Avenue in the old car barn, Dutch would get there as quickly as possible. His first move was to get the patient under cover. Because of his careful survey of the area, he hardly ever had to carry a man for more than half a block. He could always find a place to duck into quickly. Quite often, Dutch arrived after the policeman on the beat had collared his man. When this occurred, he would wait until after the officer had gone around a corner to the nearest call box and then pick up the inert form and carry it out of harm's way. If the policeman showed no sign of leaving of his own volition, Dutch had a few stratagems to distract attention. Two friendly bums would create a diversion up the street, or a breathless youngster would arrive with a tale of mayhem that had to be looked after immediately. Once the officer turned his back, Dutch would be gone with the bum. The children and the other bums always greeted this performance with a great deal of glee and, as the tales spread, other people entered into the game. It was from this practice, of course, that Dutch derived his nickname, The Body Snatcher.

Once Father Dutch had his patient safely out of sight, he could decide what to do next. Drunks present a lot of problems. In addition to being hard to handle, they fall down and break arms and ribs. They cut and bruise themselves. They have heart attacks, strokes, throw fits, bleed, and vomit. They defecate on themselves, expose themselves, commit nuisances in public, and bang their heads against walls. They drool, spit, and have vermin. In most cases, they are not conscious of what they have done or are doing to themselves, nor would they care if they realized.

Because he had received some medical education in his missionary training, Father Dutch possessed an elementary knowledge sufficient for diagnosis of the more common catastrophes that befell his patients. The first thing he did after getting a man to a sheltered place was to give him a fairly thorough examination. In the course of almost three years, he once estimated, he had found about 100 patients who were suffering from severe injuries or ailments. One thing he never tried to do was to treat a man. When he found a man who needed medical attention, he tried to make arrangements at once for that care. Probably because he was a Catholic, he most generally sought help at St. Clare's Hospital which was nearby, but he also tried to get assistance from other institutions, although not from Bellevue if he could make other arrangements. While he had no doubt as to the excellence of Bellevue's medical accomplishments, he was eager to provide something a little more personal for his men. He maintained that nothing should be done to drive them further into isolation from the world.

After determining that a man did not need medical attention, Father Dutch would look him over rather carefully, estimating the job to be done. He noted whether his charge needed a shave, new clothes, a bath, a haircut. He rarely tried to move him from the place to which he had been carried, but instead let him sleep off the effects of his drinking where he was. Out of the money from pan-handling, Father Dutch had acquired several old pillows and army blankets which he had stored in fifteen or twenty widely separated places around his district. He would bring a few of these and after first removing all his clothes, cover the patient. He stripped his man for two reasons. He wanted no shoe laces, belts, or tight clothing to wake him up, and he didn't want the man to leave un-til he'd had a chance to see and talk to him again. Dutch usually got back at about the time the man woke up, but there were many times he didn't. During the first year of his mission, the West Side of New York had a surprisingly large number of naked men reported wandering the streets. It must be rather disconcerting to wake up in a strange building with no clothes and no recollection of how you got there.

From a great many charitable agencies, Father Dutch had acquired a large stock of discarded clothing. On his second visit he brought with him a complete change of clothing, a thermos jug full of hot water, a basin, soap, and a razor. When it was possible, he tried to talk the man into coming back to his little room, but if there was an objec-tion, Dutch saw to it that the man was washed and shaved anyway. Dutch was not above getting his man down on the floor and administering the razor himself if necessary. A good deal of the time, the man would be so shaky he couldn't shave, in which case Dutch did the honors in a gentler fashion.

Whenever it was possible to get a man back to the bakery, Father Dutch could do a much better job of cleaning him up, feeding him, and calming him down. Many bums stayed in the little room for several days, eating, sleeping, and talking with Dutch over a pinochle or cribbage game. Fifteen or twenty of the more regular cases even got into the habit of struggling over to the bakery room whenever they were in the last stages of a binge so that Dutch wouldn't have to carry them. Sometimes on a cold winter evening when they were sober, five or six of them would sit around a card table, playing some game or other while Dutch sat across the room, mending clothes or knitting. Everything he took off a drunk he tried to make as good as new. Each week he would take a bundle of filthy clothing to a laundromat on Ninth Avenue, then go through it, item by item, sewing on a patch here, sewing up a rent there. Then he would put the articles back in stock for future issue.

It was only natural that the subject of reform would come up as the bums got to know Dutch better. Never once in his whole career did Father Dutch try to talk a man into climbing out of the gutter. If the subject arose, it was the bum who brought it up. Dutch was brutally frank with his patient. He simply stated that he wasn't interested in reform. If a man reformed, no one was going to do the reforming but himself. Of course, there were quite a few questions that could be and were asked. These were questions that concerned physical, psychological and moral aspects of alcoholism. Whenever these questions were raised, Dutch would tell his man that he didn't know the answers, but if the man really wanted to know, he could find out. In the course of his five years in New York, Dutch had come to know a great many social workers and psychiatrists. Any man interested in reform was sent to one of them for advice and help. That was as far as Dutch would go.

There were a great many things that Father Dutch wanted for his mission. He wanted better facilities for serving food, and he wanted more beds. At the top of his list of needs was a shower bath. The bakery manager told Dutch, in the summer of 1955, that he thought a stall shower might be forthcoming by fall, but before work on it began, help arrived from a new direction. It was inevitable that some of the men who passed through Dutch's misión would reform, and it was also inevitable that they would be impressed by the way they had been handled. At about the time the plans for the stall shower were being discussed, three of them got together with the bakery manager and formed an organization which they called the Friends of Saint Dutch. They quietly set about visiting a few monied people to raise funds for the establishment of a mission in a vacant store building on Tenth Avenue. It was to be remodelled to include three showers, a dormitory with ten beds, a laundry, and a fairly modern kitchen.

Father Dutch never heard of the Friends of Saint Dutch, and the plans never came to fruition. On the evening of November 4, 1955, Dutch carried a drunk into a vacant warehouse on 61st Street. The man, it developed, had delirium tremens. Dutch stayed with him for more than an hour and then slipped out to get his patient some water. When he returned, he found that the man was running around on the fourth floor of the building. He had pried open the doors of the elevator shaft and was threatening to jump in. Father Dutch, in trying to stop the man, was pulled into the open shaft and plunged five stories to the bottom. He died the next morning in St. Clare's Hospital.

In the subsequent investigation, Father Dutch's true identity was learned. There are a great many stories still circulating about Dutch in his former mission area. The drunks there insist that Dutch has been canonized by the Church or is a candidate for canonization, though the local officials of the Society of Jesus prefer to remain silent about the case for the present. Meanwhile, the bakery manager seems to have taken up the rescue job. In any event, the drunks insist that Saint Dutch has returned to earth, and is still snatching them from under the noses of the police.

The Free Man

Around Union Square the regulars classify Ernie Clay as a "defensive lecturer." By this they mean that he is something like the National Guard, ready to protect the citizens against the bombardments of the invaders with soap boxes. Most of the speakers at Union Square expect to be challenged and Ernie obliges.

Ernie Clay has been around Union Square for six years now. He is a tall, well-built Negro, in his early forties, with a mischievous look in his eyes and a devil-may-care attitude. In some quarters Ernie is known as The Finger because of the way he uses his index finger to strengthen his arguments. He points with it, jabs his opponent with it, waves it in the air, and smacks it into the palm of his hand. He is so adept that most crowds watch rather than listen to the argument. Some speakers, unable to compete, have just thrown up their hands and walked away. One grabbed the finger and bit it one day in a frenzy of frustration. This episode eventually ruined his career as an orator. He usually lectured on the Chase National Bank. From that day forward, however, he was known as the-man-who-bit-Ernie-Clay, and every time he showed up in Union Square, the regular audiences would shake their heads and laugh. He was good for comedy; he was no good any more for economics.

Most of the people who sit around on the benches in Union Square keep a close eye on Ernie Clay. When he gets up, throws his sweater over his arms, and strolls in the direction of a speaker, an audience begins collecting at once. Ernie will put on a good show. He is a masterful comedian. Everything is calculated to take the crowd's attention away from the oration. Often, he will pretend to

have a speech impediment. He will answer his opponent
with every word he can think of that contains an s. Before
long the target of Ernie's attention will have his hand-
kerchief out, wiping away the fine spray. At other times
Ernie will pull an American flag out of his pocket and
wave it vigorously. He has a big, red bandana handker-
chief and can blow his nose so loud and so often as to
drown out all other sound. If the speaker is making a
show of erudition, Ernie will use the same words as are
used against him, but stumble over them, purposely mis-
pronouncing and misusing them. The speaker corrects
these mispronunciations, clarifies the meaning, and even
helps Ernie get them out. By the time this has gone on for
a little while, the meeting has degenerated into a lesson
in syntax while the crowd grins in appreciation. Union
Square has its share of really clever orators who do not
readily fall for these shenanigans. If Ernie encounters one
of these intelligent men, a good debate may ensue. It
makes no difference what the argument is about, or which
side he is forced to take—Ernie is able to marshal enough
facts to prove any point he wants to make. He was once
involved in one of Union Square's most famous debates.
He and a scholarly looking bum, who wore a homburg and
pince-nez, met every day for almost a month to argue the
subject of reincarnation. Ernie was forced to a position in
support of this belief.

"I had to go up to the Public Library every afternoon
and read for three hours," Ernie explained to me. "I just
couldn't seem to get the jump on him. One morning it was
raining so hard that I had to get in off the street so I decided I'd do some extra reading. I went up to the library
about ten o'clock. When I walked in, here was this Doc
Charlie reading the same book I was reading. Only he was
three chapters ahead of me. We both got to laughing so
hard about it that we never did finish that debate. Old
Doc's dead now, but he was one of the best friends I had
down here. Sometimes when I'd start badgering a guy,
Old Doc would come over and get on the guy's side, just
for the hell of it. He was a professor of Napoleonic history
out in Ohio, or someplace, before he got on the bottle, but
he was pretty good, even when he was three quarters
shot. In fact, he was better. He was funnier."

Ernie Clay is no slouch, himself. At Oregon State College, from which he graduated in 1932, he was a member of Phi Beta Kappa, and a star athlete in football and track. At one time, in the Thirties, Ernie was a detective on the Chicago Police Force, specializing in juvenile work in the colored neighborhoods. During World War II, he was one of the first colored graduates from the Engineering Officer's Candidate School and ended up as a captain in one of the companies that worked on the Lido Road. For five years after the war, he worked in a new field. He was a portrait artist, and a very successful one. In 1949, at the peak of his career, he earned more than $30,000 in commissions, most of it coming from one of the country's largest and most respected foundations.

No one seems to know why Ernie moved from midtown Manhattan to Union Square in 1951. He is a bum by preference. Although he drinks, and has gotten drunk on occasion, he is no alcoholic. He is honest and dependable. He is neat in appearance and his disposition extremely likeable. He chews no political bones of his own in public, even maintaining what might be called a neutral stand on racial segregation and discrimination. He has argued on the subject in Union Square, but he gets no more worked up over it than he does over anything else. Some people who have contemplated the riddle of his presence on a park bench have attributed it to marital infidelity on the part of his wife. Others seem to think he is rebelling against something. If the cause lies somewhere in his past, Ernie has never said one word about it.

"I just want to be free to live, say, and do the things I want to," he says. "As long as I'm doing what I'm doing now, I've got that freedom."

Ernie Clay doesn't confine himself entirely to Union Square. He has had a verbal war going in Washington Square for the past two years. Occasionally he will saunter down University Place and rekindle the fires under the caldron. His first visits to the foot of Fifth Avenue were made in the hope that he could play an undisturbed game of chess, but he soon discovered that the park there, and neighboring Greenwich Village, are hotbeds of smugness.

"I've never seen so many people who know so much," he has said. "I decided to puncture the whole damned lot of them all at once."

Ernie declared his war on the artist's colony of the Village during the annual spring sidewalk exhibition in 1955. While wrestling with some especially abstract meanings in paintings on display, he picked out one very officious looking artist and declared aloud that art was completely outmoded by the invention of color photographic film. It made the artist in question so angry that Ernie now repeats it to artists every time he gets a chance. He says, for the benefit of his listeners, that there is nothing they can do that a camera can't do better. It is doubtful whether Ernie really believes this, being an artist himself. To further his fight with artists, he has gone to considerable lengths. When he had some money, early in 1956, he purchased a small but fairly good camera. Sometimes he invades an art class armed with this and takes color pictures of the subject from various angles. In the fall of 1956, he attempted to display several enlargements of these in the sidewalk exhibit, and very nearly precipitated a full scale battle between a group of his supporters from Union Square and one small colony of Washington Square artists. He has lost no opportunity to further the battle. He grew a ferocious looking beard similar to several which blossom on the streets of the Village, then dyed it a brilliant green. He walks up and down the streets of the Village with an exaggerated version of a beret perched on his head. Ernie is a self-appointed watch dog.

He also studies beggars closely, making periodic visits to the Times Square area where these characters abound. He misses no opportunity to expose and ridicule a fake when he finds one; he is much more adept at this particular art than are many of the detectives on the New York Police Force. He is an enemy, also, of many street corner preachers. He maintains that almost half of those practicing on Manhattan Island have no purpose in mind when they hold a meeting other than taking up a collection. Ernie is a close student of the Bible, and has made it his business to know a little about most of the various sects that hold street meetings. When he is bored with Union or Washington Squares, he will go for a long walk up Broadway or into Harlem. Whenever he finds a preacher on a corner, he will stop and listen long enough to make sure whether the man is legitimate or not. If he finds a fake, he usually sets up some kind of competitive meeting and draws the crowd away.

The mere fact that an organization is legitimate and well meaning does not save it from Ernie's "protective" measures. In 1953, Jehova's Witnesses held a big encampment in Yankee Stadium to which thousands of members of the sect were attracted from all over the United States. During the early morning hours, while most people in Manhattan were on their way to work, the streets were lined with Jehovah's Witnesses who were selling copies of the "Watchtower," and handing out pamphlets. Some of the Jehovah's Witnesses were persistent, to say the least. On one occasion a man followed Ernie for three blocks, arguing with him. This wasn't a very good thing to do. The next morning Ernie showed up on Broadway with seven or eight inebriates he had rounded up. They were in possession of several hundred pieces of literature on alcoholism that Ernie had found. Every time some overly persistent Jehovah's Witness made life a little too miserable for a person heading for the subway, he would find himself confronted by a drunk with a pamphlet on the demon alcohol.

"Some of those Jehovah's Witnesses were pretty flabbergasted when they found themselves standing there in front of God and everybody with literature of that kind. Some of them were pretty insulted," Ernie recalls. "But it never seemed to enter their minds that the people they were accosting might be insulted, or annoyed, too. I thought they needed to be taught a lesson in common courtesy, and I saw to it that they got my stuff, whether they wanted it or not."

At present, Ernie is engaged in a campaign against hawkers of merchandise in subways. Certain unlicensed salesmen of buttons, cheap fountain pens, candy, and shoe polish have been invading express trains at stations where a long uninterrupted run is in prospect. With what amounts to a captive audience, they run off a spiel that includes a good deal of tasteless and tactless loud talk. Sometimes they will make life so miserable for the meek people in a car that these poor souls buy some merchandise just to get rid of them. Ernie has a troupe of small boys who ordinarily play mambo drums and do acrobatic tricks in doorways on 42nd Street. They are backed up by two unemployed and usually inebriated trumpet players, plus Ernie himself. All of them periodically take to the sub-

ways with the sole purpose of running the obnoxious salesmen out of New York. When they track one of these
individuals into a car, they wait until the train and the
spiel starts. The boys start playing the mambo drums and
tumbling, the trumpet players tune up and eventually get
off a few good notes. Ernie sings, and he is not a good
singer. It only takes two or three rides in this company
to convince the salesman that he is done for the day. Their
number is diminishing fast.

In addition to running campaigns to do away with
phonies and nuisances, Ernie spends a considerable amount
of time giving advice and comfort. Many of the vagrants,
and quite a few of those on the fringes of vagrancy, come
to sit with him on his park benches. Ernie is a born
optimist, and he seems able to impart much of his optimism
to others. He does this simply by letting each person know
that he is among friends.

"People, most of them anyway, aren't afraid to face dan-
ger. What they are afraid of is facing it alone," Ernie says.
"When I find a guy that's pretty far down in the dumps, I
just try to show him that any problem he has has been
faced by others thousands of times. If a guy has stomach
trouble, there isn't much I can do except to point out that
a hell of a lot of other people have it, too. Ring Lardner
had stomach trouble. So did Eisenhower. This doesn't
eliminate the stomach trouble, but before long my man
realizes that he has company. He stops thinking about
committing suicide and decides to live with it. You'd be
surprised how much of a change this makes in a person."

Ernie Clay has two major possessions. The first of these
is a small wooden shoe shine box which he keeps with him
virtually all the time. The second is a large drawing tablet
which he usually carries around with him in the evenings.
His day begins around nine o'clock in the morning when
he appears on 14th Street for the first time, strolling along
with his shoe shining equipment swinging from his hand.
By eleven he has probably wandered back and forth between Third Avenue and Eighth Avenue two or three
times. His objective during this walk is to shine three
pairs of shoes. He is rather aggressive about soliciting
and sees to it that he gets twenty-five cents out of each
shine. He considers seventy-five cents enough to fulfill his
basic needs, and, once he has it in his pocket, his day's

work is done. He will then retire to Union Square or Washington Square to watch life go by, or he will undertake to complete any unfinished business that may be confronting him, such as the research on reincarnation at the Public Library. When he goes to Union Square, or to any of the other parks, he sits down on a bench and stretches out to relax. Before long he will be joined by friends. Most of them just want to talk or relax themselves. If a stranger walks by, Ernie takes up his shoe shine box and tries to make a little extra money. The stranger must look very prosperous, however, and must pass by at very close range; otherwise Ernie doesn't consider it worth while to disturb his comfort. If, in the course of an afternoon, he makes an extra fifty cents, he will eat his evening meal at the 14th Street automat. If he doesn't make anything extra, he will take his repast in one of the frankfurter stands along 14th Street or in the Village. The question of food never seems to have bothered Ernie. By some standards his diet leaves a lot to be desired, but, like most of his kind, he is more concerned with quantity than he is with vitamins. Inasmuch as he is well known at the automat, and at all of his other regular stops, quantity is no problem. He gets generous helpings of everything, most especially of sauerkraut, which he loves. Outside of his evening meal, two or three cups of coffee at intervals during the day complete his subsistence. Once in a while, late at night, he may drop in at one of the households where he is accepted as a friend. These households are all headed by women whom Ernie describes as his widow ladies. During these late evening visits, he and his friend will sit in the kitchen over a snack and a glass of milk. Ernie is very fond of cherry pie, and most of the widows keep some on hand.

About seven o'clock each evening, Ernie will take up his shoe shine box and head for Greenwich Village, stopping along the way to pick up his big drawing tablet which he has left with someone, and to enlist the services of one of several small boys whom he knows quite well. He carries the drawing tablet himself; the boy the shoe shine box.

Until curtain time each evening, he and his companion stand outside one of the off-Broadway theaters. After eight-thirty they take up a position in front of one of the village night clubs and stay there until midnight. The boy solicits shoe shines from the patrons as they arrive and is allowed to pocket any money that he takes in. When the boy gets some business, Ernie stands or squats on his haunches at a respectful distance and draws a rapid charcoal sketch of the customer. When the shine is finished, Ernie steps up and presents the sketch. The patron usually flips Ernie a coin for his trouble. On an average night the take will total a dollar. The proceeds go into what he calls his "rainy day pocket"; it corresponds roughly to a savings bank. Around midnight he shoos his companion off to bed, leaves his drawing tablet somewhere, and goes to bed himself.

Until two years ago, Ernie slept on a bench in a small park on Eighth Avenue, just below 14th Street. A crime wave that struck the city in 1954 caused a change in his living habits, however. Nowadays the police have instructions to run everyone out of a park after midnight; Ernie is dispossessed. He finally located an old woman, a caretaker to an apartment house, who needed help. Simply by agreeing to cart her garbage and refuse containers out to the curb on pick-up days, he has been allowed to sleep in the basement. There he has made a bed on the floor out of an old Navaho rug and two or three blankets. This is home. It was supposed to have been temporary until such time as he would be allowed to reinhabit the park again, but in view of the fact that there has been no noticeable change in city law enforcement trends, the basement has become about as close to being permanent as anything that Ernie knows. He still follows the same rainy day routine he established many years ago. On inclement nights, he dips into his rainy day pocket for enough money to get a bed at a flophouse on Third Avenue. With a fairly comfortable nook waiting in the basement, the expenditure of seventy-five cents is a gross extravagance, but he explains that the day will come when the basement will not be available any more, and he does not want to become too dependent upon the arrangement. Besides, he told me, sleeping in a bed, now and then, is good for him.

Like most bums, Ernie has to change his routine of living when winter comes. The outdoor sleeping season in New York City extends from mid-April to late in November, leaving about four and a half months in which a vagrant must either head south or take to the missions. When O. Henry wrote about a bum named Soapy who sought to have himself committed to jail for these winter months, he was not creating a fictional character. It is a fairly common practice, and Ernie Clay's original plan was to do exactly that. In his first year he threw a brick through a show window on West 57th Street and got six months, with time off for good behavior. The experience cured him. He found that he was not an honored guest. He was a prisoner and was not treated with the consideration he expected. He speaks of it as the biggest single mistake he ever made, and he has not tried to repeat it. In subsequent winters he tried a number of different expedients. In 1952, he lived in a room on East 9th Street near Avenue A.

"The damned place was full of bugs," he told me. "The guy in the room next to mine wanted to talk all night, and the guy upstairs thumped and banged around. I couldn't sleep when I wanted to. There was always somebody in the bathroom so I couldn't use it when I wanted to. And the landlady was always badgering me for money. Not one of these things ever happens to me the way I usually live. I have my privacy and my peace and quiet, and I like it that way." In 1953, Ernie spent the winter months in a flophouse.

Ernie took care of himself almost all winter in 1954 on the proceeds from a commission a friend secured for him. He painted the portrait of a woman who was something of a social leader in the Gramercy Park area. It was not a happy arrangement, however, because Ernie didn't like her and she didn't like him.

"The hundred bucks I got wasn't worth it," Ernie says. "At seventy-five cents a throw, I was only able to sleep in a flophouse for 133 nights. Besides that, it could have ruined me for Union Square. This old dame had more wrong ideas than any bum who ever walked into the park off Fourth Avenue, and I couldn't open my mouth to set her straight for fear of losing the hundred bucks. That's the first step towards slavery."

One of the things that Ernie doesn't tell about this particular painting is a story that has become part of the folklore of Union Square. Although he couldn't talk back, he did do a pretty fair job of deflating his subject. When he finished the portrait, it turned out to be a representation of the most penurious, hard-bitten old harridan ever seen on canvas. There was quite a long argument before Ernie collected his money.

"I painted her just exactly as I saw her," Ernie says. "When I'm not even allowed to do that any more, I quit." He hasn't done a portrait since.

Beginning in 1955, the basement quarters removed the necessity of making other winter arrangements, and Ernie has been able to live the year around without interrupting his busy schedule.

The routine of Ernie Clay's existence leaves a lot of small details uncared for. Things like laundry, shaving, bathing, and other everyday needs are provided by his widows. Ernie became acquainted with them through their children. The boys who carry his shoe shine box in the evening are drawn from one or the other of the families. Quite often Ernie will dip into his rainy day fund to buy a small bouquet for one of them. All know that a dollar spent for six yellow roses may mean that Ernie will have to go to sleep without a meal, and they often repay this little thoughtfulness with somewhat more than proper appreciation. Ernie has free access to their homes. He is apt to come or go at any hour of the day or night. Chores classified as men's chores he assumes, and he also often takes over as a baby sitter in hectic moments. Ernie's normal attire consists of a blue denim shirt, dungarees, a pair of sneakers, and a baseball cap. Each of the widows maintains a clean set of clothes for him and sees to it that his socks are darned, buttons sewed on, and that the old black sweater he wears in chilly weather is kept mended. All of the women have expressed a willingness to marry Ernie, who was divorced some years ago.

"That would sure complicate things," Ernie said, when I asked whether he was interested, "and I'm just doing my best to uncomplicate things. I'm afraid the answer would be no, although I love and respect every one of those ladies."

Ernie Clay has very definite plans for the future. He has been working for quite a long while on a pet project. He thinks, and he is probably right, that he would be quite a sensation on one of the current major quiz programs. In between reading history at the Public Library, and carefully working up a letter that will arouse interest in his potentialities as an erudite bum, he is carefully deciding which program he will honor with his presence. His decision has nothing to do with the amount of money involved. His reason for going on the program is to deflate the quizmaster. Over a long period of time he has come to the belief that these individuals are his mortal enemies. His trouble, right now, is that he can't make up his mind which one he likes least.

"What will you do after you're done with quizmasters?" I asked.

"When I finish that job," Ernie grinned, "I have my eye on several other things. I don't think this job is ever going to end."

A Lot to Go Around

Sam Victor is a prodigious man who weighs well over 250 pounds and has a huge belly that protrudes like the cowcatcher on an old wood-burning locomotive. When he moves along at a brisk pace, he resembles nothing so much as a boxcar swaying at excessive speed over a rough roadbed. Like most overweight men, he has trouble with his dress. There never seems to be enough cloth to go around. His shirttails hang out, and he wears his trousers in a precarious position below the stomach. On hot summer days there is always a good possibility that his navel will be showing just above his belt buckle.

He is a powerful man with broad, muscular shoulders and a forearm like those we used to see on baking-soda boxes. When I first knew him, we were both working in produce on the waterfront, and Sam could outlift anyone in the warehouse. It was a matter of pride with him that he could carry three or four more crates of grapefruit on his hand truck than anyone else. He was able to do it in the morning when he came to work, and he was still able to do it after he'd been on the floor for ten or twelve hours and was competing against the night shift. Victor was a sort of king around the warehouse.

He was also just about the best-natured man I have ever met. He was only a generation removed from gypsy forebears, and his swarthy complexion was always punctuated by a wide, flashing grin. The most important word in the English language to him was friendship. In its name, anything was forgivable. He expected friendship to work both ways. In all the time that I knew Sam Victor, he never maintained a home of any kind. I've since decided that the primary reason was the simple fact that Sam didn't want to offend people by leaving them to go to bed. He just didn't want his companions to think that he didn't like their company. Of course, he didn't expect anyone to leave him, either. After I'd known Sam for a little while, I always took the precaution of arranging for people to call me to the telephone around midnight. If he heard that my apartment was on fire I could get away from him; otherwise an argument would start that would last the rest of the night.

It wasn't at all unusual for Victor to stay up all night for three or four days in a row. I used to worry about this when I first knew him. During the rush periods at the warehouse, he would come to work at five in the morning. As often as not, he would still be hard at it at nine or ten in the evening. When he finished work, he would throw his coat over his shoulder and walk across the street to one of the neighborhood bars for a drink. Everyone knew Sam after he'd been in any locality for a while, so he was able to find a few congenial souls around to keep him company. He would shoot pool, play shuffleboard, and drink until the bar closed. If the other patrons happened to leave before closing time, Sam would wander down the street to a flophouse and fall into a bed for a few hours, but if he was still in the bar at four o'clock, he would just drop into the nearest restaurant, eat a big breakfast, and show up at the warehouse in time to punch in at five o'clock.

I don't think it ever entered Victor's mind to miss a day of work. He wasn't especially loyal to our employers. He just liked money, and it was a matter of principle to get as much as he could. He was especially fond of overtime. If he started to work at five, his eight hours would be up at two in the afternoon. After that he would start getting time and a half, and that's what he wanted. If it had not been for existing laws, and the fact that the warehouse closed for a few hours, he would have been quite happy to work the clock around. His pay rate was somewhere between $1.75 and $2.00 an hour, and there were many weeks, even at this rate, when his take-home pay amounted to as much as $180. In the slack season at the warehouse, Victor went out and got a second job. In the time we were co-workers, I rarely knew him to work fewer than sixteen hours a day.

It should not be assumed that Sam Victor was trying to become a wealthy man. He had to make a lot of money to keep going. For every day that he made $35, he spent $36. I've always thought that money baffled Sam. At odd moments during every week, he would become conscience stricken and begin filling up long columnar pads with figures. He would scribble away, muttering to himself and scratching his head. He would always start out by figuring out how much money he would have coming to himself on payday, then project these figures well into the future. He always seemed to be trying to find out how long it would take him to save $1,000, and was continually drawing up budgets to accomplish this feat. His budgets were fantastic affairs that were all income and no outgo. On one I saw, he planned to save $168 a week out of a $175 pay check. He had allotted himself one dollar a day for food and absolutely nothing for lodging, transportation, or other incidental expenses. At the time that I saw this particular budget, Sam was drinking two cups of coffee, eating a piece of cake and two sandwiches, drinking a bottle of pop, and eating a dish of ice cream, in about that order, during his morning breaks. This alone came to around $1.25.

A lot of his money went out in pure charity. No one ever asked for a loan without getting it, even if Sam was flat broke. If someone asked for a dollar he didn't have, he would borrow a dollar from someone else so that his petitioner wouldn't have to go without one. He never kept track of loans he made. If someone paid him back, by chance, he'd immediately stop whatever he was doing and spend the whole repayment in treating his benefactor and anyone else who happened to be at hand. It was a moment of celebration and the drinks were on him. Of course, he expected reciprocity. If he didn't keep track of what people owed him, he didn't expect others would keep track of what he owed them. It is doubtful whether he ever paid anyone back. At lunch hour he would treat everyone in sight, and run up a bill of a dollar for coffee alone. Then when it came time to pay, he would reach in his pocket, assume a blank and then a surprised expression, turn to the man next to him, and borrow a dollar. The man could hardly refuse after accepting his generosity. He would notice a coke machine, reach in his pocket, fumble around, then turn to whoever was closest and say, "Hey, let me have a dime for a minute until I get a bill changed." He was always leaving his money at home on the dresser (he got away with this at least once a day, despite the fact that everyone knew he didn't have a home, a dresser, or any money), and he was adept at the pitiful approach. He could look sadder and hungrier and more martyred than anyone I ever knew. He would stand around at lunch hour while everyone else was eating, empty handed and forlorn, waiting for some kind-hearted soul to ask him what was the matter. He'd end up with everyone pressing money on him. Three or four months before I left the job, I decided it was about time to save some money and made up my mind to get tough with Sam. I made it a set rule to say no to him on any and all occasions. I followed this policy grimly, so conscientiously, in fact, that it elicited unfavorable comment. In spite of this rigorous routine, I lent him $22.65—a nickel and a dime at a time. It is my feeling that Sam Victor could have taught psychologists a great deal about conditioned responses. Of course, his whole financial operation was complicated by the fact that he sometimes was tapped for a loan himself before he ever got the money he borrowed into commercial channels.

Sam Victor gambled on everything, but he only lost money on horse races. At one stage in his career he had been a professional gambler, running such games of chance as roulette wheels, dice tables, and blackjack games in establishments all the way from Havana to Las Vegas. He knew every trick of palming dice and stacking cards that was ever invented. He was so good at it that he absolutely refused to engage in this type of thing when in the company of friends, but if he received news of a big operation along the waterfront which seemed to be fleecing the common man, he would invade it and clean it out. As far as his friends were concerned, however, his main interest lay in more modest channels. He loved pools and usually had three or four of them going on any given day. He had them on baseball games, prize fights, the number of grapefruit that the warehouse would handle in a given day, the number of grapefruit that *he* would handle in a given day, and how many cups of coffee would be sold out of a machine in the vestibule. You could get in these pools by paying anything from a nickel up to five dollars a chance.

The main thing, as he said, was to have a little something going for you.

He made from $15 to $25 each evening at shuffleboard or pool or pin-ball at a dollar a game. He was the best pool player I ever saw in my life, and he had reduced the barroom type of shuffleboard to a science. From the time he walked into a bar until he left it, he was enthusiastically engaged. Other regular patrons rigged up handicaps to slow him down, but he always stumbled through to win. I have seen him, on good nights, playing cribbage, shuffleboard, pool, and checkers, all at the same time, and all at a dollar a game. He won every one of the contests. It was typical of Sam that he always felt he had no right to take any money he won outside the bar in which he won it. If he couldn't drink it up himself, he would spend it on his vanquished opponents. At least once in each evening, he would buy a drink for the house.

But Sam Victor's one great passion was horse races. I think he was the only man I ever met who confidently expected to make a fortune at Jamaica Race Track. I have never been able to figure out exactly what his goal was, if he ever had one, but at various times I heard him remark that he wanted to come home some night with $5,000. Now and then, he would up this figure if he had something like a restaurant that he wanted to buy. Whatever it was, he never achieved it. The last time I saw him he had had a string of fifty-five straight losing days. Each day he visited a track, he went with the knowledge that his luck was about to turn. Sam had a system that he followed religiously. He bet on horses that owed him money. If he'd bet on a horse in the past and it had lost, it was said to owe him money. The only trouble with his system was that nearly every horse in the United States owed him money and sometimes three or four of them would be running in the same race. Inasmuch as Sam always went to the ten- or fifty-dollar windows, this was always an expensive proposition. I once asked him why, if he had to bet on more than one horse in a race, he didn't bet two dollars or five dollars. He told me the lines were always shorter at the ten- or fifty-dollar windows.

It was a good idea never to go to the races with Victor. I tried it once. I took $20 and Sam took $130. By the end of the third race he was broke. At the end of the eighth race I was broke, even though I'd had four winners during the afternoon. Sam had wheedled and borrowed all my winnings from me. I remember that at one stage he gave me his lucky pieces, two silver dollars, as security. At the start of the next race after that he got the two silver dollars back and bet them, on the grounds that they were a liability to have around.

In the off-season, when the New York tracks were closed, Victor bet with bookmakers every day. He had developed a passion for five-horse show parlays. It never seemed to occur to him to bet two dollars on one horse. "You'll never get rich that way," he would say. He has never yet had one of his parlays come in so it appears that Sam isn't going to get rich his way, either.

While I worked at the warehouse, Sam Victor was consuming a fifth of whiskey a day during working hours. He would bring in a bottle every morning, stick it in the pocket of his Mackinaw, and nip at it all day long. By any other standards than Sam's, he would be called an alcoholic. Yet I never saw him drunk in all the time I knew him—unless he was *always* drunk. He once told me that he had started drinking when he was ten years old. His father and two older brothers worked in a steel mill in Youngstown, Ohio. After a hard day's work, it was the family custom to sit down at the table with a bottle of whiskey. Hard work deserved hard liquor. It evidently had never occurred to anyone that whiskey might be bad for a growing boy. If he was old enough to sit up to the table, he was old enough to take his nip along with the rest. His later career did nothing to reduce his exposure to strong drink. When he was seventeen years old, he was signed to a contract with the Cleveland Indians baseball team, and for the next twelve years he spent his afternoons in the ball park and his evenings in cocktail bars.

After closing out his career in 1941 with the Philadelphia Phillies, he bought a bar and ran it for five years. His basic code implied that it was an insult for a man to turn down a drink, and there is no record that Sam Victor ever insulted anyone. He estimates that it was during this period that he learned to drink a quart or two of whiskey a day without becoming inebriated. There have been ups and downs in the consumption since, but it still averages out to almost a quart and a half. His drinking has ruined at least one of his marriages, but not because of any effect it had on him physically.

Late in 1949, he married a wealthy woman in California. He was given the run of several exclusive clubs where he was allowed to sign chits for drinks. In the first month of his marriage, he ran up a total of $687 in bar bills. This is a remarkable sum when one considers that he drank most of this liquor all by himself. He was new in California and didn't know anyone. The next month, after he got acquainted, and started to buy other people drinks, his wife divorced him.

According to Sam Victor, he never intentionally married anyone. Yet he has acquired six wives. Two of these, whom I have never met, are presently lodged out of New York. From what I have seen of the other four wives, however, the first two probably love him very much now that they are no longer married to him.

He came to New York, in the first place, in search of Nina Axworthy, his third wife, who had gone off to Reno in protest over his bar bills. Her heart had softened to the extent of writing him a letter with $100. When he got the letter and saw the New York postmark, he hurried down to the bus depot and bought a ticket. Unfortunately, New York is a big city, and he had no address. It took two years to locate her.

Sam Victor arrived in New York on Labor Day, 1950, flat broke and with no possessions but the clothes on his back. He considered himself a bartender, and found a job in a rather run-down, decrepit establishment in the neighborhood of Avenue B and 9th Street. He did not remain a bartender very long. Next door to the bar was a small restaurant, owned by Eva Mullin, a full-blown, provocative looking widow of thirty-six or -seven. She used to drop in at the bar in the morning and again in the afternoon for a shot of whiskey. She had a way of talking back to Sam in his own idiom, and he liked the glint in her eye. Eva noticed that the bar had begun to show astounding signs of life the minute Sam Victor had put on his apron, and it was obvious that many of the customers were coming in to talk to the new bartender. It wasn't long before Eva found out that Sam was living in a flophouse and, being hospitable, she simply invited him to become her house guest for a few days. It was only a question of time until he had moved from the bar to the restaurant, where he acted as cook and waiter.

Victor had never cooked a meal in his life before, but that presented no obstacle. All the restaurant served was hot sandwiches, made hot by pouring gravy over them. But Sam was an experimenter, and on his first day he concocted a Swiss steak. He made his dish by dumping every available vegetable into a pan on top of some meat, then covering it with a couple of bottles of miscellaneous sauces. The result was nothing less than a phenomenon, and it soon became famous in the neighborhood. The taste was unusual and delightful, but the way Victor served it was even more wonderful. Because he liked to eat, he assumed others did, too, so he heaped every plate as though he were serving an honored guest. The sight of these heaping platters of Swiss steak almost broke down the East Side grapevine. Within a month from the time Sam took over the kitchen at Eva Mullin's place, the tables were jammed from morning to night. He tried other things, of course. He cooked hams after rolling them in a concoction of mustard, brown sugar, fruit juices, and assorted spices. He also invented a meat loaf. While he was doing all this, Eva was hiring new people and talking about expanding.

Just when Sam married Eva is still a little obscure, but it was around Christmas time in 1950. He'd been trying to think of some nice Christmas present, and the best thing he could think of was himself. The marriage didn't last, primarily because Sam didn't like to be nagged. Very soon after he and Eva had joined forces, the formality of his weekly pay envelope had been dispensed with. If Sam wanted to go next door to the bar and have a drink, he'd stop by at the cash register and take fifty cents. Despite the fact that he did this several times a day, the leakage wasn't noticeable because there were more half-dollars coming in than there ever had been before.

The real trouble started with a bookmaker. If the bookmaker was eating in the restaurant, it was only right that Sam keep the wheels of commerce going by placing a few bets in return. At first he began placing two-dollar bets each day. These soon grew into five-dollar bets. This was bound to make itself felt, sooner or later. Eva wasn't a very tightfisted business woman, but she always knew where she was at the end of the week. When she noticed that the profits were shrinking, she began to keep track— with only a few plaintive words at first—just when the Jamaica Race Track was preparing to open its doors for the year.

For three straight days after Jamaica opened, Sam dipped into the till for $50, which he left on Long Island. It was more than Eva could stand. This time the words were loud and vitriolic, and she locked the cash register. She began doling out money in amounts she considered proper, accompanying her largess with long and painful lectures. That was more than Sam could stand. He stayed out of sight, more and more, and finally disappeared from bed, bar, and restaurant in May, 1951. A month later Eva closed the restaurant for the summer and departed for Florida, where she secured a divorce.

Sam Victor's fifth marriage occurred in the winter of 1952-1953. He was then a maintenance man in a large housing project in Queens. He'd never so much as hung a screen in his life, but he was a good maintenance man anyway. What he lacked in mechanical know-how, he made up for in just plain congeniality. He also became sought after as a baby sitter, and on some Mondays did half the washings in the project. He made friends with every carpenter, plumber, electrician, and painter in the neighborhood. When called upon for the performance of some complicated task, he would ask the advice of these experts. The experts usually wound up making the repairs.

Helen Terry was secretary of the rental office, a virginal, strait-laced spinster of thirty-six. She was proper in every sense of the word, homely of countenance, but possessed of a superb figure. Over a period of several months, Sam's masculinity, generosity and good nature, and tales of adventure took their toll. Helen had a hope chest and other assets. She had a beautiful apartment, furnished with her own household goods, a brand new automobile, and a little better than $5,000 in the bank. Sam kept company with Helen for two or three months and then, out of the goodness of his heart, took her down to City Hall and married her.

Helen Terry may have been warned about Sam and thought she could reform him, or she may have been entirely naive. Sam claims that he was the one to be disillusioned. On the first morning after their marriage, Helen suggested that he eat the bacon with his fork instead of his fingers. A little later, when he was washing down his coffee with a slug of vodka, she asked if he didn't think it would be better to wait until later in the day to start drinking. As time passed, Sam discovered other vexations. Helen had heard, somewhere, that a successful marriage depends upon doing things together. It wasn't long before Sam realized, with some horror, that this meant *every-thing* as far as Helen was concerned. When she was un-successful in easing him into an easy chair with a pair of slippers, she began going out with him on his rounds. She even insisted in taking part in the pool games and shuffle-board matches and proved to be the one handicap Sam couldn't overcome. He began to lose money. He began hiding from her. The marriage ended in divorce in August, 1953, but Sam had left home long before that.

Sam Victor's last marriage took place in the spring of 1955, long after I had left the warehouse. My information is that she is already an ex-wife. In time, no doubt, she will take her place in life as the others have done, for Nina Axworthy, Eva Mullin, and Helen Terry are closer to him these days than they ever were when officially tied to him in the bonds of matrimony.

Sam found Miss Axworthy—his third ex-wife—again in the spring of 1952 while he was wandering around Bloom-ingdale's trying to find his way out of the East Side sub-way. She had rented a well-appointed apartment in the upper Sixties and seemed to be lonely. She took Sam home to her apartment and ministered to him. The reconciliation was fairly complete, but it did not result in a remarriage. Neither Sam nor Nina wanted this especially. She had dis-covered that he was something to be taken in small doses, and has since taken him that way. There is little question that the two are genuinely fond of one another. He did errands for her, gave her advice, and was something of a protector for her. At odd moments he would send a dozen roses to her, or invite her to spend an evening out on the town when he knew she was depressed. In her turn, Nina showered presents on Sam. On a Saturday, she would ac-company him to the races, and furnish him with money. Whenever she felt that he looked especially seedy, she would take him in tow and buy him a new suit of clothes.

She took an interest in his health and, although she always seemed to realize that there was nothing she could do to stop his drinking, she did manage to get him on a diet of sorts that periodically took off twenty or thirty pounds.

While Sam was married to Helen Terry, there was a lot of talk about his going into business. Helen volunteered to put up her savings as a down payment on a small bar or restaurant. On his days off, Sam began looking around for a good place to buy. He thought first of the bar on Avenue B. His visit there occasioned his first reunion with Eva Mullin since the divorce. She had come back from Florida and settled down to running her place as in the pre-Sam days. On the morning when Sam arrived, wearing a new suit that Nina Axworthy had just given him, and with some of Helen's money in his pocket, Eva was in the bar having her usual morning drink. The sight of her ex-husband, all dressed up and obviously in possession of new resources, wiped out a lot of bad memories. After several rounds of drinks, he ended by cooking one of his famous Swiss steaks. The sight reminded Eva that she was dissatisfied with life as it now was. It wasn't long before Eva's place became a refuge from Helen. Eventually, Eva was named corespondent in Helen's divorce suit. Sam still spends several hours a week at the restaurant, giving his ex-wife some pretty sound advice, advice which has brought about the establishment's expansion and prosperity. When in a mellow mood, Sam goes into the kitchen and does the cooking, but even when he is not actually there, the help he has trained follow out his recipes. Eva is his preferred bar companion. She is an excellent pool player, knows how to play poker well, and is a good two-fisted drinker. Her apartment is one of Sam's favorite places of relaxation. He often moves in for a week or two at a time. These days, he never tries to help himself in the cash register, but, like Nina, Eva has become extremely generous, giving him presents and helping out with the extracurricular expenses, $50 or $60 at a time.

Sam Victor's reconciliation with Helen Terry took place at the time I was working with him at the warehouse. He was suffering a rare period of discouragement with horseracing. He decided that he might never win $5,000 in a single afternoon simply by parlaying his bets. The best way, he decided, was to go to the track and bet $1,000 on a five to one shot. This involved saving $1,000. Sam, however, had a hard time saving anything. Banks were no good because they were too accessible. He would put money in on Monday and draw it out on Tuesday. He resolved to give it to someone to keep for him, someone who was preferably tough and hardhearted. At that particular moment, Helen Terry seemed to fit that description. She was prim and efficient, and he knew, from watching her in her office and at home, that once she set her eye on a goal, she never relented. Furthermore, she lived at the end of the subway in Queens. Sam went to see her one Sunday afternoon and, after much arguing, she consented. After that he took his check out every payday. Three or four months went by, and he finally figured he had about $1,100 in his fund. One day he called her up. He'd be out to get it on the next Saturday morning. He had just the horse for the 5-1 shot.

Helen Terry had changed considerably since he had lived with her. The change was mostly his own fault. A woman who had waited all her life for a good marriage, who had planned for it, saved for it, and dreamed of it, only to have it end in disillusionment, was bound to have become disillusioned herself. Helen had now taken to drinking heavily. She had learned to gamble and had become somewhat promiscuous. When Sam arrived that Saturday morning to get his $1,100 he found her drunk. He managed to get her under a shower and sober her. She then handed him a big stack of worthless pari-mutuel tickets. She had bet his entire bankroll as fast as he had brought it to her. Sam muttered about this for a long time afterwards, but money didn't mean as much to him as he pretended it did. Without much flurry or fuss, he went to work to save Helen from the ruin she seemed headed for. He was kind to her. He knew what she wanted in life, and he began teaching her how to get it. During the winter of 1953-1954, when the horses weren't running, thus leaving his Saturdays free, Sam spent much of his time with her. They wandered through the midtown shops, picking out clothes that would show her off to good advantage. Sam even took her to an exclusive hair stylist's and spent $50 of Nina Axworthy's money getting the best possible hair-do. He even talked her into having her upper front teeth pulled to improve her appearance. He made quite an attractive woman out of her. She is now an accomplished hostess, an inveterate theater-goer, and often spends her evenings in café society. Sam is probably the most important thing in her life. She keeps a bathrobe, slippers, and pajamas ready for him at all times. He visits her in Queens periodically on week ends and on cold winter nights.

Sam Victor is presently employed as a special messenger for a large manufacturing concern in nearby Long Island. It allows him to get in all kinds of overtime. He lives as he did when I first met him. During the week, he sleeps wherever there is a place handy, if he sleeps at all. He eats more, drinks more, and spends more than anyone I ever knew. On Saturday evenings, when there is no more work to do and there are no more unfriendly horses to worry about, he probably retires to the home of one of his former wives. There he relaxes, often sleeping for thirty-six or forty hours, getting ready to advance on the world again. He maintains a complete wardrobe at each place and probably still keeps a suitcase of clean clothes at his place of employment as he used to do when he parked it under my desk at the warehouse. I asked him how long he expects to be able to keep up the pace.

"Shucks, son," he said. "I'm just getting into gear."

Party Girl

Probably the only person in New York who is not worried about anything is Helga Darten. She has no job worthy of the name and no desire for one. She has tried dress designing, the only field in which she has ever professed any interest, and, having tried it, seems content to rest on her reputation. She could get married, but she's already tried it. She has become instead a party girl.

Helga came to New York in 1947 as a dress designer. She had graduated from high school that summer, gone to Dallas and got a job at the stocking counter in Neiman-Marcus. She held the job for ten weeks, then took her savings and bought a bus ticket to New York. The first day in the city she walked up Madison Avenue and, after calling at several shops, landed a position as a dress designer in one of the small, exclusive, women's stores. Her only references were a few employee identification materials from Dallas, and three drawings of smart-looking dress patterns. The job lasted just nine weeks. At the end of that time the proprietor of the store had learned that Helga not only had not designed any dresses, but that she wasn't likely to. He fired her. She hasn't held a position in New York since.

Today, Helga is twenty-seven years old. She is a natural honey-blonde with long, straight hair that is always done up in the most fashionable manner. She is fairly short and has a full figure that seems a little inclined toward hippiness. She has the traditional peaches and cream complexion, the high cheekbones, broad face, and wide, saucer-like, blue eyes of the Hollander, but her speech still has much of East Texas in it. She always dresses tastefully, whether she is lounging in her apartment or dining out in New York's best restaurants.

It should be emphasized, at the very beginning, that Helga's morals are about average. She is not a prostitute, in any sense of the word. She has achieved her present comfort through an assiduous application of certain standing operating procedures which are sometimes handed from working girl to working girl in New York. It is true that she has gone a little beyond some of the methods used by other girls, but her own devices are nothing more than an extension of them. The two simple axioms of life in the big city, for a girl who wants to live a comfortable existence, are to get as many free meals as possible, and to find a roommate to share the rent of an apartment. It was through one of these roommates that I came to know Helga.

Helga makes between $170 and $200 a month, and banks about $150 of it. Virtually her only expenditures are for taxicabs and hair-dos. Her income derives from the dress designing, which she still continues, and from rent, with a few dollars coming from other business ventures. To Helga, however, dress designing is not exactly what the phrase implies. She pursues it only for the purpose of maintaining her reputation. Such money as she gets is strictly incidental, and she has no real desire to become successful. In an average week, she will draw between thirty and forty designs. Of these she sells around fifteen. She gets one dollar for each design that is accepted, a figure that would be considered absurd if it were known to her friends, but it satisfies Helga. Her approach to the work is offhand. She simply curls up in the corner of the sofa in her living room at odd moments and draws up her designs when she has nothing else to do. She works with a drawing tablet, pencil, crayons, and five or six fashion magazines. The sketches that she makes rapidly on her tablet are almost exact duplicates of those she sees in the magazines. She adds a bow here, and a belt there. She changes the buttons from one side to the other, or puts the neckline from one dress on another. Sometimes she takes an ultra-fashionable model and turns it into a dress for a little girl. Sometimes she takes a little girl's dress and transforms it into an ultra-fashionable model. She usually

In the summer of 1954 I had to leave New York and I did not return until 1956. One of the first people I tried to find was Kennebunc. I thought he would be interested that I was doing a book and intended to put him in it. He was nowhere to be found on Third Avenue. I finally began asking a few people about him. One patrolman from the Thirteenth Precinct knew all about him. It turned out that Kennebunc was not quite so clever as he thought. Several policemen knew, all along, that he was living on the fire escape behind the theater. They kept an eye on it, out of habit, but never bothered him. When he failed to appear for several days in the winter of 1955-1956, one policeman climbed up to see if he was all right. Kennebunc was dead. At Bellevue, a day or two later, doctors officially ascribed his death to malnutrition and exposure.

One of the officers who stood around while I was talking to the desk sergeant shrugged his shoulders.

"You know," he said, "if old Kennebunc knew anybody was feeling sorry for him, he'd be fighting mad. After all, he died with his boots on and that's the way he wanted it."

"Boots on?" another officer said. "Hell, he died with his wings on. That's the way he wanted to go."

None of the other people I talked to knew about Kennebunc's death. Although the El had existed on Third Avenue long before he came there, I slowly began to realize that most of the residents along the thoroughfare identified Kennebunc with the El. One or two even had the strange idea that he had helped build it and had simply stayed on after it was finished. It was no surprise to them that Kennebunc should disappear just at the time the last girders were coming down. One day, when I was talking to a woman for whom he had washed windows, I happened to mention Kennebunc's name. A child who was playing nearby overheard it and came over to me. He told me that he knew what had happened to Kennebunc. They'd torn him down along with the El and carted him away.

changes the material and the color, using pastel shades where dark colors are called for, and vice versa. In an hour Helga will finish five or six of her designs, tossing them on the floor as fast as she finishes them. When she tires, she simply gathers up what she has done, goes through the designs, picks out the ones that she thinks have merit, and throws the rest away. The next afternoon, after lunch, she will drop the whole production at a convenient office. If any of them are bought, she accepts the check calmly. If they are rejected, she shrugs her shoulders. She sells her sketches to a wide variety of markets, mostly to the mass dress manufacturers.

Helga lives in a dilapidated old apartment building on West 46th Street, not far from Eighth Avenue. She has lived in it for seven years. The rent is $55 a month, low because of rent control and the condition of the building —the building is at least eighty years old. It has been allowed to run down badly. It is held together by magic and allowed to exist by an unusually benevolent interpretation of the building code. The floors all slant in different directions. The walls bulge and the plaster has cracked and fallen off the laths in many places. On the fourth floor, the water trickles from the corroded plumbing. On the fifth floor it drips. The walls and ceilings have been covered, year after year, with new layers of paint or thick wallpaper until there is some question as to whether the building is holding the decorations up, or whether the decorations are supporting the building. On the way up from the ground floor, every step in the five flights of stairs to Helga's apartment sags under the weight of the climber. Most people, after reaching the sanctity of Helga's apartment for the first time, go immediately to the window and look for the fire escape. One rather carefree visitor, after descending to the street one night, turned in a false alarm from the nearest corner. On a subsequent visit he posted a sign over Helga's bar, informing the guests that, in case of fire, it would take Ladder Company Number Four seventeen minutes to get a ladder up to the window.

The $55 is paid to the real estate company each month by Helga's ex-husband in accordance with a separation agreement. There was a time when her ex-spouse balked at paying rent, even letting a month or two go by. Helga packed up and threatened to move to a $250 a month hotel apartment. Investigation of the agreement by attorneys revealed that nothing was said about how much rent the husband had to pay. It also revealed that the agreement was unbreakable. Since then Helga has had absolutely no trouble. Acting on the theory that $55 is better than $250, the ex-husband keeps the rent paid up several months in advance.

Helga's father also pays her rent every month. At least he sends her the money for it. Several years ago, one of her sisters came to New York for a convention. It was a year or two after Helga's separation, and the 46th Street apartment had already been acquired and refurbished to some extent. When she heard that her sister was going to stay with her for four days, Helga went to the charwoman who had the fifth floor rear and traded flats for the duration of the visit. The charwoman was desperately poor and had nothing much in her rooms but a chair, a table, a cot, a sink, and a skylight. Helga's sister slept on the cot and primped before a broken mirror each day before attending her convention. She was horrified at the squalor in which Helga lived and lost no time in telling her father about it. After a long exchange of letters in which Mr. Darten tried to get his daughter to come back home, Helga convinced him that she had a good "career," and if she had a little financial help, she could put aside some money for furniture and other amenities. Her father has been paying the rent ever since.

Helga's roommates have also each contributed to her income. Each, in turn, has paid her $55 a month under the impression that the rent is $110. This figure is not nearly so exorbitant as it might seem. In addition to its central location, the apartment is now beautifully furnished.

In the seven years she has lived in her apartment, Helga has turned it into an abode as luxurious as anything on Sutton Place. Seventy-five hundred dollars has gone to purchase furniture, drapes, and general household supplies such as chinaware and linens, while another $10,000 has been spent for appliances, including air conditioning, refrigerators, sinks, cabinets, and an automatically controlled stove. If there is anything that has been invented lately, it can be found in the apartment. The two rooms have been completely remodeled. A stall shower with its own electric hot water heater has been installed, not to mention a completely new plumbing system that brings water directly up from the city mains. A fireplace was put into the living room at the same time the place was replastered. One visitor, who has known Helga for a long time, estimates that it would have been cheaper to buy a house on Long Island.

Helga's apartment is the handiwork of her three devoted "fiancés." One of them is a prominent advertising executive. Another is an unusually successful broker. The third is a principal buyer for one of New York's larger department stores. In order to prevent any misconceptions, it might be added that Helga is "engaged" to all three of them at the same time and has been for severals years. None knows about the others. It might seem impossible for a person to keep three separate fiancés in the dark for more than five years, but Helga picked her men very carefully for the roles they were to play. They are so much alike in most of their basic characteristics that it is impossible to describe one without describing the others. The most important attribute they all possess is nobility. It is a Saint Bernard, mournful type of nobility. They are all sorrowful, tragic characters of the type who live by a code that is based on a combination of Emily Post, the playing fields of Eton, and the ante-bellum South. It would never enter their minds that anyone could tell them a lie. It is inconceivable that any one woman could have found *three* so completely gullible men with money, but, of course, one must realize that Helga turned down a lot of prospects before she chose them. Aside from their implicit adherence to the Boy Scout Law, each has one other thing in common with the others. He is separated, but not divorced, nor is he likely to be divorced. Helga doesn't want any of her fiancés actually marrying her. The broker's situation is typical. He has a million or two dollars. If he gets a divorce, his wife will receive a substantial chunk of his fortune, but if he keeps on as he has been living for several years, he gets by with monthly payments that can be met out of current income. As he sees it, whether wisely or not, the best thing is to maintain the status quo. Whenever one of them weakens in this resolve, Helga points out the desirability of not disturbing one's capital. She has insured herself also by not getting a divorce either. Her own ex-husband, a broker, quite often decides that he would like to settle down, get married again, and raise a family. When this particular mood is upon him, Helga packs up and goes off with him for a few days. The reconciliation never is achieved, but neither is a divorce.

It should be understood that Helga has never had improper relationships with any of her three fiancés. This was another reason for making nobility a prerequisite. Each time an improper advance is made, the fiancé gets a lecture that suits his personality. It may be an appeal to his upright character, it may be an appeal to his vulnerability in the form of private detectives who could upset the status quo, it may be a review of the couple's past relationships in which mutual respect has played an important part, or it may be a lecture on the virtues of virtue. By now, after several years of resignation to selfless suffering, the fiancés are all trained well enough so that Helga can display some affection toward them without their wanting to hustle her into the bedroom. Without any of them realizing it, they have become part of a brother-sister relationship. This is the goal that Helga had in mind in the very beginning.

Because she has kept the upper hand, she has had a much easier time than might be imagined in keeping them apart and unaware of each other. Her lunches belong to them. She eats with one of them each noon hour, in strict rotation. In addition to the lunches, one fiancé gets the entire day on Saturday. Another gets the entire day on Sunday. Whichever one is closed out of the week end gets an evening during the week. There is no variation in the schedule once it is set. Helga quiets any grumbling by resorting to a lot of different excuses and standing engagements. She rarely tells an out and out lie. Her biggest excuse is her dress designing. She has pointed out that she must do her sketching in the evenings, and she has maintained the fiction of a hidden studio to which she retires for several nights a week. In order to protect herself in the event that she is ever caught out with another man, she has invented buyers and dress manufacturers and has told each of her fiancés that now and then she accepts a date to go out with a party. Two of her fiancés had to be cajoled into being broad minded about this latter type of activity, but Helga's long-time affection for them has convinced each one that he has nothing to fear from a casual date now and then. Of course, Helga knows enough about the habits of each one of her men so that she can steer well away from him. If any one of them ever sees her in the evening when he is not supposed to, it is because he is far off his habitual beat. Usually when something like this is about to happen, she gets wind of it beforehand and makes her plans so that paths do not cross. She has said, privately, that the big secret of her success is in devoting herself completely to the fiancé she is out with at the moment. The concern for his welfare and a certain demonstrativeness dazzle him.

It can be seen that Helga's token devotion to her mythical career as a dress designer has many ramifications beyond success. She uses it not only as an excuse in her dealings with her fiancés, but also to build respect for herself. Each of her fiancés is immensely proud of her. Each one thinks of her as some sort of Hattie Carnegie. The advertising man furnished most of the appliances in the apartment. He was "helping out." The remodeling, so he thought, was something that Helga was doing out of her profits from dress designing. It seemed such a struggle for her to accomplish this project that he delighted in surprising her with things that were readily available to him anyway. As a big advertising man, he could get most of the items at cost because they were manufactured by one of his firm's clients. Now and then, of course, on a quiet Sunday afternoon alone with him, Helga guided his choice of presents by dreaming aloud about what she wanted to do next with her apartment. The other two fiancés had the same general idea. Each one thought that he alone was "helping out."

Strangely enough, the purposes for which Helga sought out her fiancés in the first place have long since been accomplished. The apartment is now complete, and has been for more than three years, yet Helga's pleasant relationships with the men go on. These days they give her very little except the lunches and flowers now and then. Actually, there are moments when she gives them back much more than they give her. Very little of this is tangible, but her evenings and the Saturdays and Sundays she devotes to each one in turn provide them with a sense of well-being. As one of them expressed his feeling about Helga to me recently, "It is a wonderful thing to do the things you love to do best in the company of the person you love best."

The time she spends with the three fiancés represents a sacrifice for Helga. It subtracts, in some measure, from activities that have become a vital part of her existence. Generally speaking, she is restricted in her ability to circulate. In specific terms, she has lost three party days out of each week. Every success she has achieved stems from parties. Even the fiancés came to her through parties. Helga has never told anyone where she learned the two axioms for comfortable living in New York, but she seems to have picked them up within a few days after she descended upon the city. When she found out that she should locate someone to furnish dinner for her every evening, she set about the task methodically. In her view, the most important thing was to establish a wide base of acquaintanceship. A minimum of investigation proved to her that the best medium for this was the cocktail party. She began at once to wangle invitations, and, as soon as she found an apartment, she began giving parties herself, just to be sure that there were a lot of them and that she would meet more people.

She didn't have enough money for a party for twenty people, but somewhere she had met a girl who knew the answer. Right from the beginning, Helga would invite people, then ask them to bring their own liquor. She was young, good looking, and very poor. She found that it seemed to young and handsome men a very pitiful thing for a girl to be poor. They always wanted to help out, and a hint that a fifth of gin for Martinis would be welcome was more than enough to secure what she needed. With girls, she used common understanding. It was one struggling girl who was asking another struggling girl to have her boy friend bring along a bottle to help out. By the time she gave her fifth cocktail party, Helga was getting ten or fifteen bottles of liquor per evening. Only half of it would be used. The rest was clear profit.

Later on, when her stock seemed slow in building, she developed a new technique. She would invite people in for five-thirty in the evening, then concentrate on someone she knew who had a spacious and well-stocked apartment. Around seven o'clock, at the very peak of her own party, she would contrive to move the whole thing to the other apartment, thus saving several fifths of her newly acquired liquor for future use. She even had a way of getting hors d'oeuvres. Whenever she gave a party, she would pick out another girl as co-sponsor. Helga furnished the apartment and, supposedly, the liquor. The co-sponsor would work all day concocting showy platters, perfectly happy to be doing something to make the party a success. The cocktail party is still an important part of Helga's repertoire, but it is no longer used primarily to get liquor. After all, her stock compares favorably, these days, with that of the Brussels Restaurant.

She has always been an observant girl, and she soon began paying attention to the small talk that went on during cocktail parties. When she had a date she would steer him to one of the clubs her new acquaintances had confided they frequented. Once there, she began assembling a congenial group. Whenever an acquaintance entered, Helga would wave or stop by his table. She would generally succeed in attracting two or three couples by the end of the evening. About the time the first yawn was stifled, Helga would suggest that everyone adjourn to her apartment for breakfast or a snack before going to bed. This gracious offer would be accepted, and she would tell each girl, in an embarrassed manner, that she was out of eggs or bacon or bread. Would she mind stopping at a delicatessen on the way to pick up the missing ingredient? Helga knew where every all-night delicatessen was located and would send each couple to a different one. The store downstairs from her place was saved for her own escort, and she invariably dispatched him to spend a dollar or two. She rarely failed to net half of what was purchased on such occasions. Before leaving on the date, she would have compiled what amounted to a grocery shopping list. From it she planned her evening party, depending on what she needed most.

For a long time the emphasis in Helga's life has been shifting. She is now less busy collecting things than people. Because she depends so much on other people, she must constantly widen and change her list of acquaintances. Although she has money in the bank, and now has lunches and breakfasts provided as well as dinners, she cannot let go. She is following the same advice she gave to the broker fiancé. She is not dipping into her capital. Her stocks of everything are ample. Once in a while she lets a whole week pass without giving a cocktail party, and only has a crowd in on Friday nights so that she can lay in a supply of food for the week end.

Helga's whole life is based upon the principle of rotation. She is smart enough to know that she cannot go on getting the same crop out of the same people indefinitely. She has developed what amounts to a routine. Her system is based on ten people, five men and five women. Each of the five men is asked to her cocktail parties with the expectation that he will bring along an extra man and an extra girl. Each of the five girls is expected to bring two men. While this may sound a little difficult, it is quite easy for a girl to find two acquaintances somewhere, either in her office or among those who call her up for dates. It is especially easy for the hand-picked girls on Helga's list. The five central men in her system are similarly situated. The twenty men and ten women who usually attend Helga's parties, incidentally, provide a desirable balance. Before any of the nucleus of her party group become regulars, they understand that the real purpose of the get-togethers is to widen their acquaintanceship, although Helga never actually explains this fact in so many words. She simply chooses people who are unattached and looking for new connections.

At each party Helga gives there are always from five to ten new men. Some of the fifteen who are brought by her regulars are repeaters. Once a new man enters the apartment, he is carefully investigated. Helga judges each one by appearance, personality, and resources. She finds out where he works, what kind of friends he has, and how he reacts to her personally; for he is, naturally, one of the prospective providers. At each party, Helga picks out the best of the new crop, and quietly asks the sponsor to bring him back again so that she can continue her investigation. The second time he appears, Helga will begin trying to wangle an invitation to dinner. If he comes three times without offering to take her out, she drops him. Once a man has invited her out to dinner, she intensifies her probing. She tries to find out what he is interested in, whether he is jealous, and whether he can be depended upon to ask her out again. Among the other things she is interested in is whether she can handle him in moments of emotional stress. After carefully weighing him and his attributes for a few weeks, and after imparting some of her philosophy to him, she may put him on her list of five regulars. He then receives invitations to her cocktail parties regularly, and is expected to bring new blood into the arena. When he is added, incidentally, he replaces the man on the list who has been there longest, and he in turn is dropped when *he* reaches the top of the list. One other consideration influences Helga's selection. She will not add a Wall Street man to her list if she already has one, nor a writer if she has one of those. She wants variety. Of course, she is always careful to find out whether any of her men are acquainted with her fiancés. When she finds one, she steers clear of him.

Helga expects things from the girls on her list, too, but they are different things. Looks and personality are important because the girls are partially responsible for making her parties attractive to men. All of the girls who come to the parties regularly are relatively young, inexperienced, and new to New York. If one of the men upon whom Helga has a speculative eye is rerouted by one of these girls, Helga accepts the fact without too much concern. It adds to the reputation of her parties when a man falls for one of the girls and makes it just that much easier for her to get new faces.

Aside from the window dressing they provide, Helga expects the girls on her regular list to provide her with clothes. It is a simple process, brought about by the careful nurture of the dress designing reputation. If nothing else, Helga has excellent taste in clothes. Every afternoon she has little else to do but explore the big stores and the little out-of-the-way shops. When she steps into a gathering, whether a cocktail party or a dinner party, her dress always excites comment. Amongst her regulars, Helga never misses an opportunity of bringing up the fact that she is one of

New York's most famous private couturières. It is done subtly and without fanfare, but the word is spread methodically. Through this word-of-mouth public relations enterprise, demand is created.

Invariably, after a girl gets to know Helga a while, she begins to hint that she'd like to have a few dresses designed just for her. Helga will agree to furnish a few dresses for her friend. The number and variety will always be determined by the financial resources of the girl in question. The actual dresses that Helga "designs" are those old ones that she has ceased wearing. She is very careful not to give a girl any that she has worn since the girl joined the group. The proceeds from this sale go to pay for the new dresses.

Now and then an outsider—one of the girls who has been told about Helga by a satisfied customer, or one whom she meets at a party—buys a dress; but not often. On the average Helga buys and sells about three dresses a week. On each she makes a little profit, which she uses to buy underwear and a negligee to supplement the supply that her fiancés shower her with each birthday and Christmas. One of the by-products of this particular phase of Helga's activities is the fact that all of her five regular women companions have to be Helga's size. There was a time when there was a sameness about their general coloring, too, but in late years Helga has learned to do daring things with color on herself so that she can now supply brunettes and redheads from her own wardrobe.

The turnover in girls is somewhat slower than in men. Size enters into the picture, and so do basic attitudes. Every one of the five girls is potentially a roommate. Helga has to change roommates every four or five months. She feels that any longer association reveals too much about herself, and she is smart enough to know that her whole operation would be jeopardized if certain information got into general circulation. Being Helga's roommate is, on the whole, a rewarding experience. Any girl who comes to live in the apartment on 46th Street has access to food, liquor, good clothes, and attractive men. In all the ten years since she came to New York, Helga's only dissatisfied roommate was her husband. Like the others, he lasted about four months.

Helga has two or three intimate friends who know how she lives. They are girls who, for a time, used some variation of her methods. All of them have given up, however, maintaining that it is hard work and nerve wracking. One of them has taken a good job, the other two have married wealthy husbands. Whenever they meet her for a drink, they try to get Helga to live some other way. Lately, all other arguments having failed, they point out that she is getting old. She ought to be thinking about the future.

"I can't understand it," Helga told one of them, recently. "Here I am, getting more money in the bank every month, with not one but three devoted men, and a nice place to live. Why does everyone want me to change?"

"But what are you going to do when you're old?" her friend asked.

"Get older men," Helga said.

The Passing of a Landmark

After more than sixty years, the El was classed as a Third Avenue landmark. It took Kennebunc about five years to achieve the same status. I was introduced to Kennebunc through a friend with an apartment on the fourth floor of a building at the corner of 34th Street and Third Avenue. In the late fall of 1953, he came to me at work one day.

"There's a little guy over on Third Avenue who wants you to come and see him," the friend told me.

"See him? Why?" I asked.

"He wants you to write his biography," the friend said. "He was up in my apartment last night, and he came across that article you had in *The New Yorker*. He thinks you're just the man."

I don't know how many people have assured me that their lives would make interesting reading. I usually ignore them, but it wasn't long before I found out that you couldn't ignore Kennebunc. He didn't bother me, exactly, but he made life miserable for my friend. It got so that he called early in the morning and late at night.

"For God's sake, go and see him and get him off my neck," the friend said.

I met Kennebunc just before Thanksgiving, 1953. Our rendezvous was on the corner of Third Avenue and 20th Street on a cold, rainy night. Kennebunc was about five feet, five inches tall. His face had the hawklike look of Andrew Jackson, and it was dirty enough to grace an old $20 bill. He wore an old blue stocking cap and a discarded army overcoat so big that it almost swept the ground. Over his right arm, he carried a pail. He looked so disreputable that I was at a loss where to take him to sit down and talk, even on Third Avenue. He solved that problem by escorting me across the street, under the El, to a place called Beefsteak John's.

I discovered quickly that Kennebunc thought well of himself.

"Do you know who I am?" he asked, and then, without waiting for me to answer, he went right on. "I'm the guy that put the top beam in place on the Empire State Building. And that ain't all, either."

Before I got out of Beefsteak John's that night, I heard most of the rest of it. I found out that he'd been an ironworker for twenty-eight years. He claimed practically every structure between the East River and the Golden Gate Bridge as his own handiwork. He'd been at the top of the Chrysler Building, the George Washington Bridge, the Sky Ride Towers in Chicago, and the Narrows Bridge in Tacoma before any other man. He was convinced that the most daring men in the world were those who stood on a steel beam, hundreds of feet in the air, with nothing to cling to. He spoke contemptuously of me because I'd never had that privilege. He spoke contemptuously of anyone who had a lesser occupation. This included bricklayers, carpenters, or even other ironworkers who might have been forced to work a story or two below him. There wasn't any question in his mind as to who was the most daring of all these daring men. *He* was. He had been the king of every job he'd ever been on and he left no doubt about the fact that he'd had to fight for the title all the way from each subbasement to each tower. I'm a skeptic about little men who claim they can lick big men, and I voiced my skepticism. He fixed me with scornful eye and asked if I'd ever heard of dropping a hot rivet down a man's neck.

"You can always let a cable brush along a beam," he told me. "It's a matter of nerve. You got to take what these guys dish out and never let it get you. You just got to dish out better than you get. I got the nerve. None of those guys ever ran me off a job. Of course, you gotta be able to use your fists, and I can do that, too. If you want me to, I'll take you outside and show you."

There was one other thing that I learned about Kennebunc that first night. I found out he was stubborn. I had a pad of paper on which I made a few notes. When it

was almost time to close the interview, I asked him for
his full name.

"Just Kennebunc," he said. "K-E-N-N-E-B-U-N-C."

"That's a peculiar name," I told him. "Never heard it
before."

"It's one I took," he said. "In order to get anyplace as
an ironworker, you have to be an Indian, so I took the
only Indian name I could think of. I was brought up in
Vermont and it wasn't far from Kennebunkport, Maine,
so I borrowed the first half."

"Kennebunkport is spelled with a k, not a c," I told
him.

"Well, let them change their name, if they don't like
it," he said. "I ain't going to change mine."

I saw Kennebunc several times during the winter of
1953-1954. Every time I showed any signs of neglecting
him, he would start bothering my friend again. He was the
most persistent man I ever knew. In the end, my friend
had to move off Third Avenue to get away from him. As
for me, I finally gave up trying to avoid him. After a
while, I began looking him up. There was something
about Kennebunc that attracted me in spite of myself.

I was never able to tell whether half of what he told me
was true or not, so I tried to check up by talking to other
people who might know him. I'd always end up with an
entirely new piece of information, which led me still further afield. There was his presence on Third Avenue, for
instance. I asked him why he had given up ironworking.
He told me that he had licked so many men that they all
went on strike every time he showed up on a job. I found
out that he'd told another man that he'd been blackballed
by the construction industry. It turned out that one of the
duties of the "king" of a job was to defend the other men
against the contractor. If there was an injustice, all that
had to be done was to drop a steel beam from a good
height and in a strategic spot. The resulting wreckage
would soon make a builder see the light. Kennebunc
boasted that he had dropped enough steel beams in his
career to cause $20,000,000 worth of damage. In the end
it had caught up with him. Superintendents simply
wouldn't hire him any more. His third explanation for his
retirement, one that was peddled in bars, had to do with

multiple injuries. It appears that he fell off the Narrows Bridge in 1940, fracturing his skull, both arms, both legs, and seven ribs. By the time he got out of the hospital, the war was on and he was forced into the Seabees and spent three years building Quonset huts in the Aleutians. Despite the fact that they were *big* Quonset huts, they weren't good practice. When he went back to the high buildings after the war, he was never able to achieve his old time efficiency. The bosses all laid it to his fall. He was just as good as he ever was, but no one would let him prove it. I, myself, think that Kennebunc just got too old for ironworking at high altitudes, but I never voiced this opinion to him. It was a matter of pride with him that he was not old, and he showed a tendency to square off against anyone who dared to think so.

Kennebunc had arrived on Third Avenue in 1951 and he soon took up the occupation of window washing, the only job available that could get him off the ground. It started, evidently, when he found himself out of funds. He had been living at a flophouse below 14th Street, and he was faced with imminent eviction. The building was an old one, dating from the 1870's. It was situated on a corner and was six stories high. There was evidence that none of the windows had been washed since the El had been built; and so Kennebunc went to the manager and offered to wash all of them at twenty-five cents a window, the proceeds to be taken out in trade. The offer was accepted and a career was launched.

After Kennebunc finished his own flophouse, he went to all the others he could find, building up bed credits. From there he descended upon the general public. Within a year he was patrolling Third Avenue as if he owned it. His beat extended from just below Astor Place to a point well up in the Fifties. When he first started he had no safety equipment and no money to spend on any, so he hung out of windows or perched on ledges in the fashion of the old-time human flies. Two or three days after he started, he discovered that several people were standing in the street watching him work. This was enough for Kennebunc. He began introducing the dramatic into his work. Eventually, after his reputation as a daredevil was established up and down the Avenue, he relaxed his grandstanding and washed windows which were not even in plain view. He became secure in the knowledge that everyone knew and understood exactly what he was, and, although he felt it necessary to keep his reputation current, he felt no compulsion to prove it in public any longer.

He made it very plain to everyone that he was afraid of nothing, and his invitation to me to write his biography was simply an extension of the remarks he'd been making ever since he arrived in the neighborhood. His success as a publicity man can be seen by the fact that almost every resident of Third Avenue recognized that he had a proprietary interest in any problems that occurred above the first floor. A housewife who was confronted by a broken clothesline outside her fifth floor window usually dispatched someone to find Kennebunc. If a kitten crawled up into the girders of the El, storekeepers along the right of way called for Kennebunc rather than the fire department. Everyone knew that he would be mortally offended if the problem was solved without him.

When he first came to Third Avenue, Kennebunc took other jobs. He worked, for a time in 1952, as a taxi driver. It was not a job for a man with his temperament. After his fourth fist fight with truckdrivers who held up traffic on cross-town streets by stopping to unload, he was hauled into the Fifteenth Precinct station house and charged with disturbing the peace and with disorderly conduct. The taxicab company promptly discharged him. A few months later he conceived the idea of getting a job to help him through the winter. He went out to Riverdale, where he was sure no one would know him and tell of his disgrace, and took a position in a supermarket. He had not been there more than a week, however, when he began ridiculing the men and women with whom he worked. One of the butchers stood this for several days and then came after him with a meat cleaver. Kennebunc defended himself with a butcher's knife. When he and the butcher had been disarmed, they were both fired.

A great many Third Avenue storekeepers offered him work from time to time. One grocery store owner never failed to offer him $1.50 every Wednesday if he would clear empty boxes out of the basement. Kennebunc turned down the job each time. About his only work for would-be friends was in a shoe store in the lower Thirties, where he put boxes of shoes away on the shelves or rearranged stock. There was no mystery about his motivation. The ladder that ran around the inside perimeter of the shop on a track was so rickety that it was dangerous. It was just Kennebunc's type of challenge. He would teeter on the steps with great relish, balancing as many boxes of shoes as he could carry, never dropping one, never falling.

Kennebunc's decision to wander up and down Third Avenue was a free one, made from choice rather than necessity. He had a son who lived in Los Angeles and who urged him to come to California. In 1953, his son came to New York and, failing to make any impression with words, resorted to fisticuffs, administering a good beating and literally carrying the old man off. It was the only way to make Kennebunc do anything he didn't want to, but even this failed. Two weeks later, Kennebunc reappeared on Third Avenue with a new pail.

Kennebunc charged ten cents a window for his work. He arrived at this figure after a long evolution. As long as he confined his work to flophouses and took his pay in trade, he had no trouble getting twenty-five cents per window, but when he began tackling building superintendents and housewives along his route he ran into both competition and sales resistance. When his price dipped to ten cents he discovered that he had eliminated both. There wasn't a window on Third Avenue that he couldn't wash. He was completely happy from morning until night. The one big drawback was that it was economically unfeasible. No one could be expected to wash enough windows at ten cents apiece to make a living. Kennebunc multiplied the problems. While the actual process of washing a window might consume no more than ten minutes, he often devoted half an hour to testing and figuring out how to do the job without causing his client any damage or breaking his own neck. Most of the buildings were old. The window ledges, more often than not, had loose bricks. In many cases the window sills were rotted and the sashes coming apart. Kennebunc tested every brick, tried every window to see how much pressure he could put on it, and checked the putty. Only then did

he start washing. It was a matter of professional pride
that he had never so much as cracked a pane of glass, or
splintered a piece of wood. I asked him, one day, why he
didn't get some safety equipment.

"There's no building on Third Avenue high enough to
worry about," he said.

There were some days when he spent ten or twelve
hours at work and washed only eight windows because
of his careful approach. Under the best possible conditions, he rarely took in more than $14 a week, working
seven days. His average weekly income was about $10.

In his two and a half years on Third Avenue, Kennebunc learned more about the residents than anyone ever
had. He walked along the street at all hours of the day
and night, always observant. Most people were so con-
fused by the noise and shadows of the El that they never
saw much of anything, but Kennebunc never missed a
movement, especially if it was above the first floor. He
knew the children and deduced what kind of arguments
he was likely to need to pry forty cents out of their mothers for four windows. He knew that on certain blocks
all the women congregated at the neighborhood grocery at
ten in the morning. He knew that on others several wage
earners all worked for the same company and were paid
on the same day. He knew, as a matter of fact, when
most of the paydays were. When he made up his mind
that he would concentrate on a certain block, he would
go to that block, stand on the corner for two or three
hours, observing everything. By the time he was able to
launch a real campaign in that area, he knew which bars
certain people drank in, how long they drank, how much
they drank, and how much money they spent. He knew
what time the lights went out in the windows at night,
and what time they came on in the morning. From this he
deduced what type of jobs the people held and the kind
of habits they indulged in. He knew where every sick person was on Third Avenue, and where all the prostitutes
lived.

Kennebunc used his fund of information in many ways.
Quite often he would be washing windows at four o'clock
in the morning or at eleven o'clock at night. He was able
to do this simply because he knew that a customer was a

subway motorman and had to get up at that hour anyway, or that another customer never went to bed until three in the morning. The mother of four small children should be approached during one of the few times in the week when she was not harassed. Young stenographers who shared an apartment were simply made to think that there were fine lines of print in the lease requiring them to have the windows washed regularly.

At first Kennebunc continued to live in the flophouses at the lower end of his beat. When he reduced his price to ten cents, however, he had to move to cheaper flophouses, farther downtown, and eventually give them up altogether. Shelter is usually one of the first things most men require; with Kennebunc it was the first thing to go. He was used to the life of a gypsy. For twenty-eight years he had roved back and forth across the United States from one job to another, camping out in a tent, or sleeping in a trailer. When he found that he wasn't going to be able to afford flophouses any longer, he went back to camping out again, but without a tent. On the nights when he had no place to stay, he picked out some hallway or hidden areaway, and curled up in it until he got enough money together to go back to a flophouse again. He began a fairly systematic survey of every building on Third Avenue. As a window washer he had a legitimate excuse for being inside and was able to do a lot of unhindered exploring. In a year, he knew more about the structures than the fire inspectors did. He knew every court, areaway, alleyway, and air well. Wherever two adjoining buildings did not quite come together, he edged into the space and explored it. When he entered a building to wash the windows, he tried every door to see where it led. He examined the basements and the roofs. Not only did he examine the premises, he investigated the occupants of the buildings so that he would know which ones were likely to let him sleep in peace. Besides the buildings and tenants, Kennebunc studied the policemen. He didn't want them bothering him, either.

As anyone who talked with Kennebunc for more than five minutes would have guessed, the shelters he liked best were the fire escapes. They were high up off the ground, to begin with, and they allowed him to maintain the illusion that he was sleeping on a steel beam. He could look down on the world and see what was going on. He could enter or leave them without disturbing anyone. Kennebunc knew every fire escape on Third Avenue. His preference, of course, was for those hidden from the street. He found about fifty that descended on inner courts or in obscure alleyways, and he concentrated on them. From April to November, he moved from one to another, curling up on the steel grating and going to sleep with nothing much under him but an old throw rug he'd found somewhere, and nothing whatsoever over him. In the first winter of this routine, he retired either to a flophouse or to a warm hallway.

By 1951, when Kennebunc first came to Third Avenue, the television era had "arrived" in New York City. Already, between Astor Place and 42nd Street, there were a few darkened movie theaters, all with large and commodious fire escapes, three covered by sheet metal canopies. The police never gave them a second glance. On one of the theaters, two or three blocks from 23rd Street, the fire escape descended into a little alleyway at the back of the building. This one was Kennebunc's headquarters. It had three different landings, one for the orchestra floor, one for the mezzanine, and one for the balcony, the latter about four stories above the ground. This top landing became Kennebunc's home. He hauled pieces of Celotex, Balsa Wood, and other insulating materials to line the bottom and top and walls. He even fashioned himself a doorway closing off the landing from the lower part of the stairs. He had acquired several old blankets, a chair, and a rickety table. The result was a small furnished room. No one knew he had homesteaded a valuable piece of Manhattan real estate.

Kennebunc never had any money for clothing. In the wintertime he always wore the costume that he was wearing when I first met him. In the summertime, his costume consisted of a dirty white T shirt, a pair of pants many sizes too big, and a pair of sneakers. Shoes were the main problem. At one time his feet were encased in burlap bags. At another time, he decided to go barefoot, but the police soon put a stop to this. Then he went to work in the shoe store and this problem was solved. Toilet and laundry were another complication. He carried a razor in his pocket and every day he would borrow a mirror and shave, using the water in his pail. Baths, naturally, were hard to come by. He tried one or two of the public baths maintained by the City of New York, but always complained that they were uncomfortable, dirty, and lacking in privacy. For a while he used the showers in a mission, where he conscientiously left twenty-five cents in the poor box. As he became more familiar with the people and places where he worked, however, it became his habit to duck into the bathroom and under a shower in an empty apartment. Quite often, if he happened to be washing windows in an apartment with a washing machine, he would stick his T shirt in with the family wash. Now and then he was even able to retire to the back hall and get his shorts off and into the machine, too.

Throughout his life, Kennebunc's habits had been relatively austere. He kept himself in the best physical condition possible. He moved briskly and with a firm, sure step. He never drank or smoked, although he enjoyed going into a bar in the evening and bragging to the regulars. And he followed one peculiar ritual that seemed to pass for recreation. Every Monday morning he went out looking for a fight. He followed a simple procedure. He visited a few construction projects in midtown Manhattan, ostensibly to apply for a job. His appearance at these sites invariably brought forth derisive catcalls from many of the workers, and Kennebunc would stand and answer in kind. Sooner or later he would manage to be more insulting than insulted. A few blows would be struck and Kennebunc would return to Third Avenue, a satisfied look on his face.

Virtually all of Kennebunc's money went for food. He ate most of his meals at Beefsteak John's where we had our first talk. Now and then, if left alone in an apartment, he was not above looking in the refrigerator for a snack, and he made no secret about fishing for invitations to dinner, especially from some of the lonelier widows along the Avenue. A lot of people were a little hesitant to offer Kennebunc very much, however; he was so fiercely independent, no one ever knew how he would react to charity. Unfortunately, in the long run, the amount of food that he consumed was well below what he needed to live.

A Bench in Madison Square

One night in the early spring of 1953 I was sitting in Grand Central when a man came up to me and asked me if I was "up against it." He said he had noticed me in the waiting room several times and worried because the guards might notice me and invite me to leave. He had lived in Grand Central for about seven years and knew all the ways to avoid discovery, but he didn't think I did and suggested that I "go down to Madison Square and see a guy named George Spoker. He wears a bright red tie and a blue shirt, and tell him that Jerry sent you." George Spoker, it seemed, was an expert on how to get along on practically nothing.

So I went. I found him without any trouble. He was sitting by himself on a bench on the 26th Street side of the park. He had four or five gray ledgers piled beside him. Several men came up to him, one by one, talked to him briefly, and then left. I went over and introduced myself.

"Jerry sent me," I told him. He asked what I needed and I said, "Money." Had I ever worked in a grocery store? I had not. There was a store nearby that needed someone to cut cheese—was I interested? I was, and for a month and a half I cut cheese. After that, I went back often to Madison Square to talk with George. We became friends.

George Spoker is a medium-sized man with thin lips and rimless spectacles. His blue workingman's shirt and his red bow tie set off a somewhat crumpled old herringbone tweed suit. He claims he is a bum, and has lived like one for seven years, as though he were trying to prove something. It was his habit to sit on the bench in Madison Square with a pocketful of dimes and hand them out to other bums in a manner that suggested he was making an investment. He was always asking questions and, although he rarely found fault with the answers, he left the impression that he did not necessarily believe them. He was like a small-town banker who knew exactly how much money all his customers had.

The comparison of George Spoker with a banker is not at all surprising. He had been one for a good many years. He had presided over a family institution in a city near San Francisco until the examiners found a shortage in his books, after which he had been deposited in San Quentin for a period of two and a half years. He protested innocence of any wrong-doing, but he never protested very loudly.

"Every con in San Quentin is in on a bum rap," he used to say. "What's the use of trying to kid myself, or anybody else. Nobody'd believe me, anyway."

After serving his sentence, Spoker never went back home. During his prison term his wife had divorced him, his material possessions had been liquidated, and he had a bad taste in his mouth because none of his old friends had visited him. He once told me exactly why he came to New York.

"I was a bum to everybody and I made up my mind if that's what people were going to think of me, I might just as well be one. I wanted to be the God-damnedest bum that ever lived. I wanted to get drunk and stay drunk. I wanted to be the dirtiest, raggedest, most foul-mouthed specimen of manhood that ever lived."

If anyone ever walks along the street with an authority on such matters and tries to pick out the down-and-outers in the throng, he will recognize that the one earmark of a bum is aimlessness. Right at the very beginning of his career, a lack of aimlessness differentiated Spoker from his chosen colleagues. He attacked the problem of being a bum with some determination. He bustled around, walking briskly and asking questions in a sharp, businesslike manner. He worked hard at the game, putting in fifteen or sixteen hours a day. Whenever he heard of something he had not tried yet, he rushed to experience it. He was unable to shrug his shoulders and accept the things that Fate turned his way. As a banker, he had lived most of his life guided by maxims about thrift, industry, and honesty;

sayings like "Time waits for no man" were as much a part of his bloodstream as the corpuscles.

There was another big difference between George Spoker and the run of the mill: he had money. While he had been in prison his maternal grandmother died, leaving him a monthly income of $78. The proceeds from this that had piled up during the last months of his prison term had enabled him to travel east in a drawing room on an extra-fare train. He was probably the only man who ever entered the realm of the Salvation Army by way of a reserved compartment. He couldn't bear the thought of all that money going to waste, so he very carefully took out a post-office box and went to it on the first of every month to pick up his check. The way it turned out, Spoker was never really a bum at all. He was simply living on a very small income.

George Spoker did not know much about bums. He had read books about them, and he had been accosted on the street for handouts. When he first arrived in New York, he assumed that all bums lived in flophouses. He tried a few of these establishments on the Bowery, but he couldn't stand the bugs that crawled on the floor, or the smell of vomit, so he moved slowly uptown and eventually established himself on Third Avenue, where flophouses cost fifty cents a night instead of twenty-five. He tried eating at restaurants like Beefsteak John's but he couldn't stand the sight of three or four kinds of food all heaped together in one pile, so he transferred his affections to Nedick's, now and then taking a whirl at the automat. Inasmuch as one of the keystones of his new career involved being a drunken stiff, he very carefully budgeted his money so that he'd have enough to get good and drunk every Saturday night.

The getting-drunk part of it was really the thing that ruined George Spoker as a bum. He could drink enough to get drunk, all right, and very often did, but the very act of drinking led to his downfall. He soon fell into the habit of patronizing one bar all the time. It was a place called Beanie's Tavern on 14th Street, near the lodgings Spoker called home. It was a stand-up bar. The mirror was covered by signs faintly reminiscent of a supermarket. About the only thing that Beanie's never ran was a one-cent sale. There were weekly specials on brands of whiskey that the Bureau of Internal Revenue had never heard of, and the place seemed filled with disreputable-looking men clamoring for bargains. Outside, on the sidewalk, homeless men gazed hungrily through the windows at the television sets or the whiskey ads. A half dozen inebriates slept in the nearby doorways. No one ever staggered very far after leaving Beanie's. Beanie's Tavern was populated by real, honest-to-God bums. George rubbed elbows with them and talked with them, and he soon came to feel like a National Guard recruit in the presence of battle-scarred veterans just back from Korea.

"I was a dilettante," he recalled not long ago. "I was sleeping in a flophouse every night and patting myself on the back for the hard time I was having. To the guys that came into Beanie's, a flophouse was a luxury. If they managed to sleep in one once a week, they considered themselves lucky. They were spending the night on the subway, flopping in doorways, holing up in vacant buildings, cat napping in Grand Central, and stretching out on park benches. If they got any money at all, they spent it on whiskey."

The realization that he was something of a failure in the thing that he had set out to do made Spoker more determined than ever. He made up his mind to try living like these models with whom he had become acquainted. He got himself a notebook, which he carried in his back pocket. Each time he went into Beanie's and heard of a new place to sleep, he wrote it down in the notebook. Then he set out to try every one of them. He soon discovered that resting on a park bench is hard work and it wasn't very long before he found himself gravitating back to the flophouses again. Each time this happened he became more disgusted with himself and eventually reached the astonishing conclusion that he did not have the guts to be a bum. There was only one thing he could think of to do to keep himself from taking the easiest way out: that was to give away his money. He began by having it changed into quarters, which he handed out here and there.

It was at this point in his life that George Spoker's true nature reasserted itself. It was not like him to do anything haphazardly. Orderliness and system were ingrained in him. Furthermore, he could not stand giving away something for nothing. In order to satisfy both of these inclinations, he decided to trade his quarters for information. Each time he gave one away, he asked the bum to tell him where he had slept lately. This information was carefully entered in the little notebook. When one notebook was filled, Spoker got another bigger one. It was not long before he discovered that his informants would talk just as much for a dime as they would for a quarter, so he reduced his unit of exchange.

The information that went into George Spoker's notebooks was a curious marginal account of life in New York. Vacant buildings were listed according to type and location. There was data on tunnel excavations, used car lots, and encampments of Jehovah's Witnesses. One day George met a bearded old character who insisted that he had been sleeping in the sarcophagus of a French king in the Metropolitan Museum for ten years, off and on. George investigated this claim, as he did every parcel of information he received, and found it plausible, but he never quite got up the nerve to spend the night there. For over a year, however, he did sleep in a different place every night. Before he decided upon an accommodation, he studied the habits of guards or police, means of ingress and egress, and the best times of night for use of the premises.

George Spoker wandered the streets of the city for almost a year, stopping now and then to hand out a dime and interview a bum, then rushing off to investigate some new possibility. It was a full-time job, and he rarely stayed in one part of town for longer than a day at a time.

One day while he was walking down lower Broadway, Spoker was accosted by a vagrant who had once added something to the notebook. The man said he had been trying to find George for several weeks because he had been evicted from his customary sleeping place and needed a new one. He was willing to pay twenty-five cents for a look at the places George must have available. George did better than the man asked. He told his petitioner about a spot he characterized as guaranteed for two weeks of undisturbed slumber. This encounter revolutionized Spoker's life. The realization that he could sell back for twenty-five cents the same information he had received for a

dime was a new idea, and in order to take full advantage
of the possibilities the idea opened up to him, he began
telling the men he interviewed that if they ever wanted to
find him, he would be in a certain place every day at one
o'clock in the afternoon. At first this place was Union
Square, but Spoker soon decided to move his place of
meeting to Madison Square, where things were less hectic.
It wasn't long before he was giving out information on
sleeping arrangements to seven or eight vagrants a day.
He has estimated that he had a total of several thousand
hideaways when he first went to Madison Square, not all
of them current, but most of them good.

"I liked Madison Square," Spoker recalled. "It's leafy
and green. Nobody bothers you much if you just want to
sit and look up at the buildings. I came there, first, because
I had to be there every day at one in the afternoon. After
a few months I had enough customers to keep me there two
or three hours a day. I just decided that I'd had enough of
running my legs off all over town and that I would stay
right there."

George Spoker is naturally a curious and observant man.
On the first day he arrived in Madison Square he counted
the buildings that bordered it. If he arrived at his bench
before one o'clock, as he usually did, he snooped around
in these buildings, reading the directories in the lobbies
and counting the elevators, trying to estimate how many
people were employed there. He knew how each building
was heated, who washed the windows, and who scrubbed
the floors. What he could not find out by looking, he found
out by asking. He was soon eating all his meals in one or
another of the lunch stands along 23rd Street and knew the
countermen who furnished a lot of information. On rainy
days during the first winter he was in the neighborhood,
he often visited the public library to look up old newspapers and magazines published fifty or more years before, at the time the corner of 23rd and Broadway was
more or less the crossroads of the world. Whenever he
came across an event of interest that had happened in or
near Madison Square, he was sure to look up the spot at
which it occurred.

"A lot of people say that looking up bits of information
like that is useless," Spoker once remarked, "but they're

crazy. There isn't any information that is useless. I even know the numbers on the buses on the 23rd Street cross-town line."

Spoker continued to add to his notebooks for two or three years after he first came to Madison Square. In the summer of 1948, however, the information he had been collecting about Madison Square began paying off in a rather unusual way. On hot evenings he was apt to remain in the park until quite late. On one such night as he strolled leisurely around the square, he stopped to talk to a man he found sitting on a chair outside the entrance to one of the office buildings. The man was in his shirt sleeves smoking a pipe, and obviously was enjoying the breeze that stirred on the fringe of the park. It turned out that he was the night watchman for his building and had been for more than twenty years. Before that, he had been an accountant, working for a firm in the vicinity for many years. Spoker asked about some of the events he had come across in his reading, and the old man was only too happy to recall the past. It soon became George's habit to drop by and chat with his new friend every night. On one particularly rainy evening the old man, who knew by that time of Spoker's chosen profession of being a bum, suggested that his visitor stay in the subbasement all night. He even rounded up some old burlap bags to make a comfortable bed for George. From that time on Spoker lived in Madison Square. His friend soon introduced him to other night watchmen and night engineers and, by winter, George was as much a fixture in the neighborhood as the statues in the park. He went to one of the Army and Navy surplus stores and bought a sleeping bag and blankets, which he moved from one basement to another. Not all of the engineers and watchmen were interested in the history of Madison Square, nor were many of them desirous of hearing Spoker discourse, but he made it a point to become *persona grata* to all of them in one way or another. He did errands for them, brought coffee to them each midnight, and sympathized when they were in trouble.

In the fall of 1948, George Spoker stumbled onto something good. It grew out of his attempts to ingratiate himself with the building employees around the square. While going over his notebooks in the park one September day, he was suddenly assailed by a thundershower. As was usual in such forced curtailments of activity, Spoker spent his time loitering in the lobby of one of the buildings. In order to keep from being run out into the street, George had carefully cultivated the acquaintance of the elevator starter; and on this occasion he talked idly with him while the rain came down. When the interruption had passed and he was about to leave the building, he casually said he would saunter over to 23rd Street for a cup of coffee. The starter wondered if Spoker would mind bringing back a cup for him.

"I thought about it all the way across the park," he told me recently. "The man had given me a quarter to pay for his coffee and had intimated that I could keep the change. This looked like it might be a good business. I bought six cups of coffee instead of one and saw to it that each one of the elevator operators got one of them. They all paid me, and they all tipped me."

When he had pocketed his tips, Spoker began asking questions. He found out that no one was bringing coffee into the building. Within a week George Spoker had received permission from the building superintendent to bring snacks to all the building employees at regular intervals. Moreover, he had asked to be allowed to solicit a similar privilege from all the various firms that employed more than 600 people in that one building. Mathematically speaking, Spoker was no slouch. He estimated that there were 25,000 to 30,000 workers employed within a block radius of Madison Square. They would drink 12,000 cups of coffee, or partake of that many snacks, on an average day. At a nickel a snack, somebody could make $600 a day in tips, and George Spoker made up his mind to be that somebody.

From the time he had first become involved in questioning vagrants as to their nocturnal habits, George Spoker had received a lot of extraneous information that had nothing whatsoever to do with shelter. Bums often blurted out that they had eaten at some mission or other, or that a cerain charitable institution in town was a phony enterprise. The fact that there was a drunken counterman at a certain 28th Street restaurant was valuable, especially if he was dishing out generous helpings. It was a good place to send anyone for a meal, and later on it would be a good place to send someone to get a job. There was a constant stream of economic data coming to Spoker. He knew of vacancies in dishwashing departments of restaurants, and of bowling alleys that needed pin boys, and he knew who was hiring men to carry sandwich boards in any given week. He put all this in his notebook and later cross-indexed it and entered it on three-by-five cards which he kept in a discarded filing cabinet in the second subbasement of an old business building, where he was a good friend of one of the guards.

With this supplemental information George Spoker had already become something of a one-man sociological movement by the time he stumbled onto the coffee-carrying business. There is an unofficial spirit of helpfulness amongst vagrants in New York, and the word soon got around that anybody who wanted a little money in his pocket should go and see the man in Madison Square. He would not furnish any himself, but he could supply tips about where to get it.

"I knew all kinds of stuff," George Spoker recalls. "And I knew how to use it. Let me give you an example. Somebody who knew me fished a guy out of the river one morning, then told him to come down here and see me. The guy's got oil from the river on him and smells like hell. He hasn't shaved for weeks. What I mean, he's a mess. I took one look at him and I know he's been on a six- or seven-day binge and that the first thing he needs is some food in him. The cleaning-up can come later.

"I gave him a buck and sent him down to Beefsteak John's on Third Avenue. They don't care how you look or smell down there, so I knew they'd let him in the door. I told the guy to come back and see me after he'd eaten. He did. I figured the thing he needed next was a bath and some clean clothes. For the bath and shave I sent him to a mission on 15th Street. When he'd got done there, I sent him over to the Salvation Army to get some clothes. The ones they give you don't fit like tailor-made suits, and they're a little frayed sometimes, but they're clean and make you look halfway respectable. I figure that if a man wants better ones, he can earn them himself. Anyway, after the guy got his new clothes on, I sent him to an outfit that needed someone to hand out printed matter to people on the street. He earned about a dollar an hour for that. I also gave the guy a vacant store building to sleep in on Lexington Avenue. What I did for the guy wasn't much. I'm no uplift guy, so I got paid for it. I got back the buck I gave him for the food. I got a couple of bucks for getting the job for him, and I got two bits for the store. I never saw him again after he paid me so I don't know whether he ended up back in the river or in a penthouse on Fifth Avenue. It's none of my business, and I've seen enough bums so that I don't care any more."

The Spoker Aid Society, as he used to call it, became the key to his new business, and the business became the key to the Aid Society. Beginning in the winter of 1948-1949, he carefully organized a catering service in the buildings around Madison Square. He started with the building to which he had first brought coffee to the elevator starter and operators, personally talking to the heads of the various businesses and laying out a route that would keep him occupied for a full eight-hour day and pay between ten and fifteen dollars in tips. When he had the route adjusted to his own satisfaction, he turned it over to the most promising of the bums who came to him for help, taking three dollars of the tips for himself. Then he started to organize another route. At the peak of his catering career, in 1952, Spoker had about twenty men working for him and was taking in close to $300 a week as his cut from the tips.

It took George Spoker almost three years to reach the apex of his career. By that time he had branched out considerably. At first he and his men took orders from the people in the buildings and had them filled at one or another of the numerous lunch counters in the area, but when the business became big enough, Spoker looked around the Madison Square area until he found the cheapest and most obscure vacant basement there was. He rented this and set up a kitchen to take care of his own orders. His profits from this enterprise, together with his cut from the tips and a few other sidelines from which he received money, soon totaled about $600 a week. In 1952, Spoker filed a Federal Income Tax return for $31,000. At the time he was still sitting on his park bench in Madison Square and sleeping, every night, in any one of about twenty subbasements in the neighborhood. He was wearing the same blue shirt, red bow tie, and the crumpled old suit he had brought to New York. And he was still keeping most of his records in one of ten or eleven notebooks piled beside him on his bench.

George Spoker left Madison Square in the winter of 1953-1954 after selling out his business to a large catering company for a huge profit. It was not the money which caused him to give up the place that had been his home for six years; he was perfectly happy with his life as it had been. His habits hadn't changed a bit. He took one shower a week at an Episcopal mission. Whenever his one suit became too dirty or too shabby, he would take it to a cleaner's, donning an old coat and pair of pants he had received from the Salvation Army in the interim. He changed his linen once a week. He ate a sweet roll and drank a cup of coffee from his commissary for breakfast, had a frankfurter from one of the 23rd Street stands for his lunch, and ate an evening meal in the automat, usually picking the lowest-priced item on the menu. His recreation still consisted of going down to Beanie's Tavern and getting drunk every Saturday night, although it is doubtful if he ever got very drunk, because he spent most of his time circulating among the patrons getting material for his notebooks.

George Spoker had become almost the tightest man in the world with a dollar. No one knew he had money. He had kept his mouth shut. All of his routemen reported to him on his bench in the park and turned their money over to him, after which he waved his hand and told them to go and get the orders filled. He pretended not to count the money, and it is possible that he did only make spot checks. It was a wonderful opportunity for a dishonest man to cheat him, but no one had the heart. Most of the men who worked for him had been carefully nurtured on the idea that George was running the business just to give them, and others like them, a chance to rehabilitiate. It was a charitable proposition, the whole thing, and if someone cheated George by holding out on him, that someone only hurt himself in the end. So no one cheated. Meanwhile, nobody but George knew how many men he had working for him or how much money he took in. He had accounts in eight or nine banks in the neighborhood and crossed the street to one or another of them six times a day, took all the money out of his pockets and deposited it. He had no second-in-command and such bossing as was done consisted of a word of advice here and there. He left a very plain impression with each man that the business was being run so that the workers would get a break. If there was any inefficiency, the only sufferers would be the bums. There was very little suffering, because each man worked conscientiously. Spoker was also careful to let most of his men go after ten or twelve weeks. Aside from the fact that this constant turnover kept everybody in a constant state of confusion about what was going on, it saved an enormous amount of bookkeeping and office detail. As long as he didn't pay anyone more than $600 a year, George didn't have to bother with withholding taxes and social security. No·one found fault with any of these arrangements. The employees were all bums to begin with, and they recognized George as a benefactor who had given them a little time to get on their feet. After all, it should not take a man forever to get going again.

It was a woman that caused George Spoker to give up his career. He had written off the feminine part of his associations while he was in prison. The fact that his wife had divorced him after his incarceration caused him to become a little bitter about the whole sex. In addition, there is evidence that he had subjected himself to a scathing self-assessment. He was fifty years old, balding, and not exactly handsome. What could a woman see in him? He decided to become a woman ignorer, if not a woman hater.

It was inevitable that someone in a high place would learn about the man who sat in Madison Square and dispensed charity. Word eventually reached the city editor of one of the metropolitan dailies, and he dispatched a feature writer to see if something could not be worked up for a Sunday edition. George Spoker was not talking to any reporter. He had too many reasons for not divulging any vital information about himself. After fencing his way through two different interviews without saying anything important, he was suddenly faced, one morning, with a good-looking, red-headed woman of about thirty who told him a simple and rather commonplace New York story. Her name was Sarah Haddon, and she had come to town to be an actress. She had not found enough work and that morning, when she came back from breakfast, she found that she'd been locked out of her room. A friend of hers had told her that he had gone to Spoker in a similar emergency, so there she was. Sarah Haddon, of course, intended to write down everything that George Spoker said and did, then put it in the magazine section of a Sunday newspaper.

"I'd been in Madison Square for five years," Spoker said to me, "and she was the first woman that ever came to me for help. I can usually spot a bum a mile away, but I suddenly realized while she was talking that I'd never even seen a woman bum. It never occurred to me that there was such a thing. It was quite a challenge, but just how much I didn't realize until I tried to do something for her. When a guy comes up to me and asks for help, I size him up and try to decide what he needs first and most. If he's half starved to death, I get some food into him. If he is dirtier than he is hungry, I start out by getting him cleaned up. I tried to size this girl up like that. She looked well-fed and well-dressed, so I decided the thing I'd better do first was get her a place to stay. I opened up my notebook and started to thumb through it before I realized that I just didn't have any place that would be suitable for a woman to stay. I finally had to tell her to come back after lunch and I'd see what I could do for her. She was trying to ask me questions all this time about the notebooks and what I had in them, but I wasn't even listening to her. I kept thinking about the fact that I'd never seen a woman bum before and how awful it was. It gave me the creeps."

George Spoker's solution made him the first bona fide, homeless person in the city of New York who ever kept a mistress. What he did was to go out and rent an apartment for Miss Haddon. He knew of a small flat on East 27th Street that was vacant, so he paid a month's rent and even went so far as to stock it with twenty dollars' worth of groceries. In discussing his move at a later date, he always insisted that his motivation in renting this apartment was pure. Miss Haddon was simply the x in an equation that had to be solved at once, and George took great pride in solving problems. Whether this was all there was to it or not, he somehow registered enough sincerity to convince her. When she returned to the bench in Madison

Square that afternoon, he took her by the arm and led her triumphantly to her new place of residence, showed her inside, demonstrated how the stove worked, and left her alone.

Sarah Haddon, as might have been expected, was already possessed of a quite livable apartment of her own, and the presentation of this new set of living quarters put her in a difficult position. She was under the impression, along with everyone else, that her benefactor was a bum, yet the most generous man alive. She seemed to have been slightly aghast at what she had done and, for the moment, not knowing what else to do, decided that she had better accept the charity to keep George's feelings from being hurt. There ensued a period of several weeks in which she spent a good part of every evening at the 27th Street place, talking with Spoker, who had gotten into the habit of dropping around every night after dinner to see how she was making out. Each time he came he was full of suggestions, none of which were any good, and each time he came he brought some little thing in the way of flowers or food to make her drab world a pleasanter place in which to live. Sarah stayed around the apartment until he left for one of his subbasements, and then she went to her roommate with a new supply of groceries. Towards the end of the third month, when there seemed no hope that the pattern of things would ever change, Sarah decided that she had better live in the apartment that was being furnished for her, so she moved in, bag and baggage.

It would probably be safe to say that by the time Sarah decided to accept George Spoker's full hospitality, love had begun to show through the charity. Despite his own appraisal of himself, he was not entirely without charm. Sarah was certainly attractive. In the spring of 1953 Spoker began absenting himself from his sleeping bag two or three nights a week. By June of that year he was making a token visit to stay with his friends one night a week. At some point along the way, he and Sarah were married, and the secret of his true life leaked out. When it did, his wife moved her new husband to a home in Westchester.

Spoker continued to sit on his park bench in Madison Square until January, 1954. He was there every day, running his catering service and maintaining the fiction that he was a bum. No one will ever know how much money he was worth by that time, but it was well up in six figures. If there was anything he had learned in the banking business, it was the art of good investment. One rumor that got around after Spoker left Madison Square was to the effect that he had built up an income of around $10,000 or $12,000 a year, exclusive of his business. By the end of his stay on the park bench it must have been hard for George to keep from admitting, even to himself, that he was not a bum. It was probably a combination of Sarah and weariness that made him leave the scene.

"There is nothing the matter with being a bum," he is reputed to have told one of his friends, "but when you have to commute thirty miles every day there's just no percentage."

Epilogue

Just the other evening one of my friends walked through Union Square and saw Ernie Clay admonishing a befuddled speaker with his customary confidence. Some things in life don't seem to change.

Yet Henry Shelby, to whom subways were a way of life, is now teaching school in a small New York city an hour or two up the Hudson. Things weren't the same any more, he told me at dawn over a cup of coffee in an automat. "It was a little thing," he said. "The Transit Authority changed the routing of the trains on the Sixth Avenue line. You can't get south of Chambers Street on an F train any more." He had to make an extra change during the night, and his sleep was seriously disturbed. "I was just too damned tired to figure a way around it so I got all cleaned up one day, walked into a teachers' agency, and applied for a job."

This is a book without an end. Who can say—certainly not I—where my friends will be, what they will be doing tomorrow? They may give up their twilight society and live what convention describes as "normal" lives. They may not. But of one thing I am sure. They will change, as all people must, as long as they have life. Change is one sure constant in the human equation.

I've been hunting for Charlie Knutsen for months but he seems to have disappeared. Has he gone back to Iowa? Will he turn up in the list of musical and theatrical castings? Someday I may know. But if Charlie Knutsen goes back to Iowa or Henry Shelby to teaching school, there are always others to take their place. Only the other day a librarian in the New York Public Library called my attention to a young man and woman who arrived together about five minutes after ten each morning. In the library's main reading room they devour volume after volume with obvious hunger. The library has become, in a way, their home. They explore its intellectual resources and make use of the library's other facilities—they groom themselves in the washrooms, talk together quietly in the little nooks. One watches while the other sleeps. At a quarter to ten each evening they leave. I haven't introduced myself yet; one doesn't wish to impose upon people in the quiet routine of their lives. But I've watched them long enough to know that they have agreed to be homeless together. Most of the twilight people I have known are essentially lone people; this touching evidence of shared vagrancy is something new. Someday I will know more about it—or if not I, another person fascinated with the lives of people.

These are my friends. I hope others will be lucky enough to have friendships as rewarding as these have been to me.

Other SIGNET Books You'll Enjoy